INNER ANCHOR

TIPS TO IDENTIFY AND OVERCOME BULIMIA NERVOSA FOR TEEN GIRLS

SHANNON MICHELLE

TABLE OF CONTENTS

INTRODUCTION

Your teenage years are some of the hardest to endure as you wade through middle school and high school. In these formative years, we start to figure out who we are and what we want to do with our lives. Those who enjoyed high school are the minority. Everyone has struggled with some aspect of it at some point during their middle and high school years. Unfortunately, those struggles are heightened for someone who struggles with eating disorders.

Eating disorders, especially in young girls as early as nine, are rising in the United States. These disorders are not as strongly discussed in public health and are encouraged by the climates within and outside of school. Pressures of being skinny from the media, parental figures, and the student body in school are some of the causes of eating disorders, especially in the case of bulimia nervosa. However, bulimia is mainly about controlling the one thing you, as a sufferer of bulimia, can control: your diet.

Bulimia is often portrayed as a disorder where the sufferer tends to make themselves sick after eating a meal. Often, this is portrayed in film, television, and other forms of media as a joke instead of realizing that this disorder has less to do with the food itself, but more about the lack of control the sufferer feels in her life. Being teenagers and treated as such may prove detrimental to the health of someone who suffers from this disorder at such a young age. Oftentimes, they may feel invalidated and are unable to truly trust anyone who may be able to help them. Bulimia, to say the least, adds another stressor to a young girl's quality of life.

THE STRUGGLE

As a teen, your emotions are all over the place thanks to the newly found hormones surging through your body and brain. With all the newness and your body developing into a young adult, you are no longer treated as a child, but you are also not treated as an adult. The lack of a decent support system for you is detrimental; your eating disorder is now spiraling out of control, and you have no one to help you through it. Your anxiety and stress are at their peak, and you do not know how to maintain them on your own.

This lacking support system is isolating you from the family you thought you had. Shame and the inability to communicate with an open heart and mind about your issues are causing significant rifts around the people you love, such as your family and friends.

No Support From Your Parents

The secrecy of an eating disorder, especially to your parents, friends, or significant other, is a huge burden to bear. They might not even believe you. Or worse, exacerbate the situation. No one wants a crybaby. You're a teen, after all, not an adult (as many adults like to point out). You don't know the meaning of 'stress' because you don't have 'adult' problems yet.

Any attempts to have an open, honest conversation about your relationship with food are met with an eye roll or an exasperated sigh from your parents. It is all about what you are doing and not about *how* you are doing. Your extracurriculars and how well you're doing in school is your entire identity now. Your feelings of isolation are increased. This isolation has constructed a wall, an anti-teen barrier you can't pass. With the isolation comes intense feelings of depression and anger.

The off-hand jokes about your weight have taken their toll on you. Even though your family might think it's okay to joke about something that bothers you, it's exhausting to tell them how you truly feel about the jokes. Even when you do, the conversation is usually dropped.

No Support From Friends

The same can be said about your friends as well. Your friends are not blind; they can tell you're losing weight, but say nothing to you about it. Instead, they either joke about the situation, call you dramatic and attention-seeking, or completely ignore the problem.

Parties are now a no-go and bring up excess anxiety. What kind of food will be there? How can I maintain this secret part of me? What excuses can I give if I need to go to the bathroom? How often can I get away with going to the bathroom before suspicions are aroused? There are so many questions that either you're not prepared to answer, or you simply do not have the energy to make up more lies.

You're isolated at home and at school. There is no one you can talk to who will listen to you and what you need.

Societal Pressures and the Media

The correlation between success and being skinny is woven into the fabric of society. Celebrities are often young, beautiful, and most importantly, *skinny*. The same can be true of successful YouTubers, TikTokers, and other social media influencers in today's generation of teens. Never before has the younger generation been so close to the media, and therefore impacted by it.

Everywhere you turn online is a workout video, fat-shaming, or pictures of successful, thin, and healthy-looking celebrities. Those who absorb this content may often have a skewed view of society, and therefore society plays by those rules. It's exhausting to see and experience daily.

But what if I told you that, despite all the obstacles and the biases to overcome, you could become healthy again? That at a point in the future you can love your body, and yourself, more than you thought you ever could?

YOUR LIFE IN FIVE YEARS

Eating disorders require a lot of recovery processes and a complete change in your mindset. How you manage stress as well as other people's opinions about you weighs heavily on the inside and negatively impacts your external image.

But if you can, try to think about the future—say, five years from now. I know it can be difficult to think of the future right now, but paint a picture of it. Close your eyes and visualize. What do you see?

In five years, the eating disorder will become a core memory for figuring out who you are and what you want out of life.

You're in the process of pursuing your dreams—what that means is up to you.

But the most important part? You'll be healthy again, with a healthy relationship with food, your body, and your self-image. You finally know how to treat your body with the tenderness it deserves with proper nourishment and exercise routines. You have accepted yourself in all your forms both past and present. Your self-esteem has increased dramatically as you have learned to let go of all the negativity that once surrounded you. You will finally feel at peace about your weight and self-image.

So the question is: Isn't that a life worth fighting for?

WHAT WILL YOU LEARN?

With this book, you will gain insight into your eating disorder and how to best overcome it. This book is only a step in the recovery process, but it will help you beat your condition and start to live life again! Living life is the most critical aspect of life, and you should live yours in such a way that you are both proud and humbled by your experiences. This book will be kind to you through validations without offering up judgments.

This book will help guide you in the direction you need to go by providing tips to move forward, the external context of eating disorders, and explanations of the underlying causes of eating disorders. This new context will be a guide to your recovery, separating the external perspectives and internal beliefs which have plagued your mind and, by proxy, your body.

Helping you achieve recovery matters deeply to me because what you're about to learn helped me to see and understand the impacts of external perspectives controlling my interior beliefs about myself.

WHY SHOULD I LISTEN TO YOU?

This question is one that I receive a lot. From an external perspective, it might seem that I have never had an issue such as this. After all, I went to college, earned my degree, and I have a successful career. But I will tell you now, that is far from the truth. I had suffered from both anorexia and bulimia when I was a teenager, around the same age as you. I know what it's like to be in your shoes, and I'm here to validate you and remind you that you are not alone.

I moved to Gainesville, Florida, with my family when I was about 12 years old. Once I graduated from high school, I attended Santa Fe Community College, then transferred to the University of Florida to finish my degree. Throughout this time, however, I struggled heavily with two eating disorders known as bulimia and anorexia. Struggling with both opened my eyes to the impact of external and internal factors on my well-being. It was not a pretty sight to see.

I was only a whopping 92 pounds in my senior year of high school. My weight fluctuated, but the lowest weight correlated with my darkest time fighting these disorders and their mindsets. I did a lot of research and soul searching to learn everything I know now. It was bitter work, but the results of the work led me to a better path and a brighter future.

I am writing this book because I know what it's like to face the internal struggle you are battling. The pitfalls of external perceptions can affect you the most, especially in the emotional and physical state of mind you are currently in.

TAKE THE PLUNGE

Chances are, you picked up this book because you are either a teen struggling with an eating disorder, or simply someone you love is suffering from the eating disorder bulimia and you want to understand them better. No matter your interest in this book, the information contained within will help you understand the devastation eating disorders can bring. Not only that, but the causations and some tips will help guide you to the result you want to achieve.

So the question is, are you ready to take the plunge? To dive in and learn more about the world of eating disorders?

Then continue reading. The first chapter will discuss the major factor in eating disorders: the food itself. What kind of relationship do you have with food, and how does that make you feel about your weight?

FOOD VS. WEIGHT

*T*he relationship between food and your weight is a staggering influence on how you not only perceive yourself but how you perceive the food that's around you. When you do eat, what kind of food are you eating? Is it healthy and nutritious, or is it unhealthy, heavy, fatty foods that make you feel good at the moment, but then you're anchored in guilt later on?

How you eat and the types of food you consume are topics that I'm sure you're all too familiar with. Food, the body, and weight are all popular topics, and with good reason. The relationship you have with food, in general, is an insight into your inner psychology.

I want you to keep in mind that there is no shame in how you are feeling. At this time of your life, your emotions are impacting your eating habits. However, short-term emotional responses to food, such as making yourself sick, will have long-term consequences for your life.

Some people have better relationships with food, and that's fine. But that's them and you're you. This chapter is to help you understand yourself so you can ask important questions about your journey with food. With some research into the causes of your feelings towards food and your self-image, you will find that you're not alone in your struggle.

Discussing the causes of your internal struggles will help clarify your perceptions of eating. In Chapter 6, we will delve into more about talking about your emotions and how to create a steadier emotional regulation through therapy. Remember that recovery is a long process, and there is no blanket solution for everyone who suffers from eating disorders.

WHAT IS BULIMIA NERVOSA?

Bulimia nervosa, or bulimia for short, is an eating disorder that can be rooted in mood disorders such as depression and bipolar disorder. While eating disorders can correlate to also having mood disorders, this isn't always the case. It's unknown what the exact cause of the eating disorder is; however, according to the staff of mayoclinic.org, there are many reasons you can develop the eating disorder such as:

- Societal pressures
- Genetics and biology
- Excessive dieting
- Substance abuse
- Extreme stress, and
- Your emotional and psychological state (2022).

Bulimia is one of several types of eating disorders. Oftentimes, there are foundations of anxiety, fear, and the often lack of control in the personal life of the sufferer. Because of this fear and anxiety, it causes you to hyper-fixate on your body and weight. This hyperfixation about your weight suggests you may struggle with low self-esteem and self-worth.

Bulimia nervosa is the eating disorder when you secretly consume foods without control, and then somehow purge the food through various means such as:

- Self-induced vomiting immediately after eating
- Over-dieting
- Weight-loss supplements
- Exercising more in comparison to how many calories you consume
- Fasting
- Overusing laxatives
- Using enemas excessively after eating (Mayo Clinic Staff 2022).

The list above consists of some of the more commonplace purge types. It's important to note that these purge types are unhealthy coping mechanisms for your distraught feelings about your weight and your appearance.

Eating Disorders in General

Having an eating disorder is a terrifying experience and one that can be difficult to overcome without the proper support system that is needed. Just like with any other type of disorder, there is an inherent need to be understood and heard. In the case of eating disorders in general, the sufferers are unable to discuss their feelings in a safe environment. Therefore, they use this disconnect between their inability to communicate and translate it to the concept of food and food intake.

Eating disorders that continue for a long time can lead to complications later on in life. They are serious medical conditions that need to be treated as soon as possible to reduce the risks of medical complications. Some of the complications include:

- Teeth decay combined with gum disease, which could then rot inside your mouth
- Kidney problems due to dehydration
- Problems with digestion, which include nausea, heartburn, or issues with bowel movements
- Missed or irregular periods, and
- Suicidal thoughts and actions (Mayo Clinic Staff 2022).

Eating disorders are potentially life-threatening disorders and require immediate attention and action. While no one can force you to seek therapy or find other solutions, there is someone who will help and support you during this difficult time. A friend, school counselor, or someone who you trust to hold you accountable in your fight against the disorder will help you in the recovery process. Eating disorders are nerve-wracking and terrifying, especially when you try to work through your problems alone.

THE LINK BETWEEN EMOTIONS AND EATING

Many studies have been conducted about the causation of eating disorders such as anorexia nervosa, bulimia nervosa, and even obesity. Eating disorders can be defined by depression and repression of the self. Those who suffer from depression, anxiety, and other mood disorders are more prone to eating disorders as well.

Eating Disorders Are More Common in Adolescent Girls

I was only 12 when my disorder started to occur. I would eat a small breakfast, little to no lunch and would come home to snack until dinner. After eating dinner with my family, I would feel heavy and nauseous. Scowling at myself in the mirror, I judged my appearance through a harsh lens of self-perception. I used to take a stereo with me into the bathroom and run the shower simultaneously to drown out the sound of making myself sick. My stomach growled and churned as I slept through the night, but I repeated the pattern. Feeling overfull after dinner led to my bulimia which further led to being light-headed, nauseous, and ashamed. Bulimia haunted me until I received help after high school.

Studies range from various ages in young girls and women. According to Nina K. Schlacter, 'Girls as young as four talk about being fat and going on diets, words they learn from the media and from parents...and some studies report that girls as young as eight suffer from full-blown eating disorders,' (Accessed 2022). Young girls are affected mostly because of impossible beauty standards presented to them by the media, resulting in eating disorders like bulimia. However, bulimia is also presented genetically.

In a study conducted by Tatjana van Strein et. al. in the *Journal of Psychiatric Research*, it was discovered that genetics and the serotonin neurotransmitters in the brain are among the causes of eating disorders in young adolescent females (2010). Serotonin transmitters, or SERTs, are responsible for the varying emotional states of the brain. The SERTs, when inhibited or dysfunctional, cause hormonal and chemical imbalances. This leads to mood disorders and, in some cases, eating disorders.

It is critical to understand the source of your disorder. While genetics play a part, they aren't the whole picture. Sometimes, the reasoning lies behind trauma, especially in childhood.

Trauma and Bulimia

Trauma, especially in childhood, can develop into mood and eating disorders. Exposure to abuse and neglect, especially when it comes to food, translates to the need for consumption and then purging of the anchor of food. Trauma is felt in the moment, but its impacts last a lifetime.

Trauma within familial life and the dynamic of the family are one of the underlying causes of eating disorders including anorexia and bulimia. I'm mentioning this here to introduce the concept of trauma as a factor of bulimia and its impact on the inability to control emotions. However, we will be continuing the discussion of family life and its impacts in Chapter 3.

Uncontrolled Emotion Regulation

Sufferers of eating disorders are most likely suffering from various mental health disorders such as bipolar disorder, depression, and anxiety, although this is not an exhaustive list. With mood disorders comes the frequent inability to control your emotions in a healthy manner. In some cases, this can translate into food consumption and weight perceptions.

It is intriguing to note that, according to a study by Adrian Meule, when sufferers of bulimia are feeling positive emotions such as happiness, their food intake decreases. The polar opposite of the spectrum is when the sufferers are feeling negative emotions such as anger and sadness, their food intake increases (2019). When you start to feel upset, the need to consume everything grabs you. When that food is no longer sustaining your need to feel better, guilt sweeps in.

Guilty Conscience

When you start to feel the anchor of food weighing you down, the immediate need is to purge everything you've eaten. There are many reasons for the purge such as anxiety, comments about your weight, or the fear of getting fat. I remember feeling the same way when I was younger, often starving myself because of my anxiety and feeling overfull from dinner, then eating and purging all the contents in my stomach.

After devouring food while in a depressive state, the guilt you feel from the consumption of food is heavy. Then you purge. You're caught in an unhealthy cycle of eating, purging, and the helplessness that results from the issue. You want to get better; you want to feel like yourself again without the constraints of extreme dieting and the almost instantaneous need to purge what you've eaten. The feelings of guilt, helplessness, and shame are the revolving doors in your head. These emotions and feelings are the results of the negative emotions you feel.

Negative Emotions Spell Disaster

Negative emotions are the gateways to an unhealthy relationship with food for someone who suffers from bulimia nervosa. Intense emotions such as fear, sadness, and anger are detrimental to you; they cause you to consume the food you enjoy the most. The weight of the food, both physically and emotionally, makes you sick. This extra weight you're carrying is the result of unrealistic expectations that have been set on you.

You're trapped in this vicious cycle, but it's a part of the cycle that only you can control. In my experience, my life was preset and deviation from the norm was often frowned upon by my parents. I was numb to it all. I had no control over my life, but my diet? *That* was something I could control.

THE ONLY CONTROL YOU HAVE

Your life is essentially planned out for you right now. Your parents control everything you do, and you don't have that much say in it. You might be involved in extracurricular activities that you don't particularly like but would look great on a college resume. The types of classes you take are dictated by the school and what your parents think is the best option for your life after high school. Your interests, however, are on the back burner in the grand scheme of your life.

No matter the type of socioeconomic background you hail from, there is always a degree of control from parental figures or guardians. Whether your family is wealthy or only scraping by, the constant dictation over your life gives you little power over what you can do with it.

You're trapped in a cycle of deep unhappiness and an unfulfilling life. Eating disorders are about control because you have none anywhere else in your life. Take a minute to reflect and understand how this lack of control manifests in you and what you're currently experiencing. Is it your parents and their unrealistic expectations of you? Is it because there is something amiss you can't control? Dig deep within yourself to find the answer. Once you find the underlying cause of the lack of control you feel in your life, it will be easier to reestablish the things you can control.

Currently, what's the one thing you can control? How you view your body and therefore, the diet you give yourself. My diet and how skinny I looked were the things I could control.

The Constant Analysis of Your Body

Every time I passed a mirror, I looked over my body and focused on all its flaws. I'm not talking about the presence of acne, but how my body looked in my clothes. I was always checking myself in the mirror to see if my clothes looked good on me. I always thought, 'My stomach is too big,' or 'My thighs are too thick.' In reality, my body looked healthy, but my mind told me I looked fat and gross.

Because of feeling like this constantly, I used to weigh myself before and after showering. I often lifted my leg onto the tub wall so I could analyze in the mirror whether my thighs were too thick or not. During my analysis of my legs and thighs, I also looked at my waistline and turned to the side to see whether my stomach was too large.

The constant overanalysis of my body didn't stem from vanity. I wasn't comfortable in my own skin because of the heaviness I felt after eating. What I didn't know was how serious of a mental and physical health problem I had. I didn't realize in my middle school and high school years that I had a problem. Eventually, this type of overanalysis became routine for me.

You're in a constant state of analysis of your body, which is both exhausting and unhelpful to you. This constant analysis of your body then slips into the constant analysis of food.

The Constant Analysis of Food

When you think about food, the only thing you can think about is the need to control your weight and the excess fat on your body. This type of thinking can drastically increase feelings of guilt, shame, anger, and sadness. You're in this constant state of mind where you believe you need to examine everything about dieting and food.

The common misconception about bulimia nervosa is the need to purge food after eating. Bulimia can also manifest itself as the excessive need to count calories or exercise. How the disorder presents for you personally will vary between you and another sufferer of bulimia nervosa. In either case, anxiety surrounding food types and their impact on your body are uncontrollable. After eating, you feel heavy, weighted down, and are especially perceptive to how your clothing fits.

The anxiety surrounding the unhealthy relationship with food reveals itself in physical symptoms. The obsessive need to count calories and exercise unravels itself, making its presence known. On top of counting calories and exercising, there are physical ailments that can be present as well.

My eating disorder manifested in making myself vomit at the end of every meal. I always felt nauseous, and constantly making myself sick led to me being nauseous during dinner time. I forced myself to eat smaller bites to be able to get through dinner at all, even in restaurants. To combat the heaviness in my stomach, I ordered caesar salads for dinner as a way to eat something light that wouldn't upset my stomach as much. Caesar salads would be all I ate for the next several years when my family and I went out to eat.

Uncontrolled Anxiety

Waves of nausea pass over you. Your head is swimming; your stomach is knotted from your constant state of anxiety.

Nausea subsides now and again, but the sickly feeling never leaves you. Concentrating on anything is difficult.

Your chest is constantly tight and burning from the anxiety and the ever-present acid in your stomach. Your chest is on fire while your stomach thunders its need for food.

In addition to the nausea are the recurrent headaches and dizziness from not having a sustainable diet. The headaches and dizziness alone are causes for concern, especially when you're in the middle of class and need to focus on the lesson. You can't concentrate, and you lose focus on what needs to be learned.

Not only is uncontrollable anxiety an issue in school, but the constant anxiety wreaks havoc on your digestive system.

FOOD TYPES AND THEIR IMPACT

Think about the last time you ate something and were able to keep it down. Was it something light on your stomach and easily digestible? Foods containing a minimum amount of calories and carbohydrates minimize the need for purging under some circumstances.

You might think about how the last time you ate steak, it made you feel nauseous. When preparing to eat with your family, you instead opt for pasta, believing that it would help curb your nausea. However, the contents of the pasta you just ate are also way too heavy on your stomach. It sits there without digesting, causing you to feel sick. Now you must go purge it out, to keep the queasiness at bay. Not only is the physical weight of the food sitting in your stomach, but the feelings of unhealthiness are there too.

Heavy Foods

Think for a moment about the types of food you eat when you binge. Are they high in fats, sugars, proteins, salt, and carbohydrates? Or are they usually highly processed foods? If you said yes, chances are you're eating heavy foods. These are the types of foods that sit in your stomach, ordinarily causing you to be sluggish, fatigued, and bloated. These foods take a lot longer to digest than lighter foods. Your body is taking longer to process the nutrients you need from the food to provide the energy you need. Some examples are:

- Pasta, which is heavy in carbs;
- Bread, which is heavy in carbs;
- Meat and protein such as cuts of chicken, pork, beef, etc.;
- Dairy such as butter, milk, cheese, and ice cream;
- Desserts like cakes, pies, and cookies; and
- Potatoes are also heavy in carbs.

While these foods aren't inherently bad for you, they are entirely dependent on how they're prepared and what types of ingredients are used. For example, mashed potatoes are combined with dairy products such as milk, butter, and depending on the recipe, are mixed in with cheese. While mashed potatoes are delicious, if the meal is combined with a heavy serving of meat and no vegetables, it will give you that feeling of sluggishness and heaviness. This could result in a purge because of how long that particular food type sits in your stomach. Meals often partake in the combination of many heavy foods.

Fried foods are also a culprit for experiencing heaviness in your stomach. Deep-fried foods are a staple in our modern culture, but they can have devastating health effects further down the line. Because a vast majority of appetizers and sides to a meal are deep-fried, this leads to more heaviness and feeling nauseous. Every time I eat fried food, it makes me feel heavy. As a result, I tend to refrain from eating these types of foods.

Light Foods

Light foods, in vast contrast, are foods that are easily metabolized in your system, and therefore much easier to digest. They feel light on your stomach, and you feel much more energized in general. These light foods are fruits and vegetables that can be made into salads or as a side to a meal.

Salads can still be light even with the inclusion of other heavy foods. For example, a caesar salad often has grilled chicken, croutons, and cheese included in it. However, this salad is also light on your stomach, and you're still using some of the heavy foods to feel fuller. It's essential to have a balance of different types of foods, especially during your recovery process. You will feel healthier by having the necessary nutrients for your brain and body. You will also feel lighter if you have a balance of both heavy and light foods in your meals.

While the foods listed in both heavy and light foods are guidelines, it depends on how you feel after eating. For example, a fruit salad can feel heavy because some fruits have complex sugars and higher sugar content such as:

- Cranberries,
- Pineapples,
- Figs,
- Bananas, and
- Pomegranates.

When fruits are dried, they also have a higher sugar content than fresh fruits. The water in the fresh fruits balances the sugar content. This will also prevent any heaviness in your stomach caused by the dried fruit.

Beverages

Beverages can also cause heaviness in your stomach while also giving you a bloated feeling. Not only can there be excessive sugars in your food, but the same is also true for your drink of choice. Cutting down on unhealthy beverages can help you regain some control over your stomach and your purging. Some of these beverages include:

- Milk,
- Teas,
- Orange juice and tomato juice,
- Soft drinks including diet soft drinks,
- Carbonated water,
- Processed juices, and
- Coffee.

Due to the high sugar content especially in soft drinks and processed juices, some of the drinks listed can cause bloating and an increased heaviness in your stomach. Milk is a part of the dairy category, which can contribute to feeling gross and then purging. While orange juice and tomato juice aren't especially heavy per se, the elevated acidity in these beverages can also be attributed to feeling queasy. If you're an avid coffee and/or tea drinker, the caffeine alone is enough for your stomach to churn and even have spasms.

When I purged, I often drank orange juice, which helped to settle my stomach. I'm not exactly sure why it worked, but it did. As I mentioned, the foods and beverages listed above are simply guidelines. What you eat and the amount of it is at your discretion because it depends solely on how heavy you feel after consumption.

While water is the best solution for maintaining bloating and feelings of nausea, it can also be bland. You can add the flavors you enjoy or find ways to incorporate water in other beverages such as lemonade and other light flavors.

Fast Food

We all know that fast food is bad for us, but sometimes the necessity is there. In between busy schedules, not knowing how to cook, or feeling drained from the day, fast food is an easy choice for many because of its convenience. But this convenience is costly to our bodies.

While it's best to avoid as much fast food as you can, it may be necessary at times. However, this food is also causing you to feel this heaviness in your stomach as you eat it. Fast food is loaded with excessive salt, fats, preservatives, and other factors that cause you to feel bloated, sluggish, and sick, especially if it's a constant factor in your diet. But you can slow down on the intake of fast food by preparing more meals that are necessary for your recovery.

TAKE CARE OF YOUR BODY

The most important thing you can do for yourself is to take care of yourself, including your mind and body. You'll read about what to do to calm your mind and take care of your mental and emotional states in Chapter 6; but for now, let's focus instead on your body.

You may have heard the phrase, 'Your body is your temple'. As cliche as it is, there is an underlying truth to it. To properly care for your mind, you must first take care of your body by supplying it with the nutrients it needs. This can be done in small steps by supplementing your current diet with additional hydration by drinking water. Water can even enhance the taste of your meals!

Remember to start small and work your way up. If you can hold down, for example, a salad, try to find ways to incorporate other ingredients into it such as nuts or other proteins. Having steak or grilled chicken will help enhance those flavors as well. Trying different oils, types of vinegar, and salad dressings will help keep the meals from repeating, and therefore growing bored of them. Don't be afraid to experiment to find out what taste and texture pairings are right for you and if you can stomach them without purging.

Food Is Life

It's imperative to slowly increase your intake of heavy foods. You don't want to shock your system by implementing numerous changes at once because you might relapse into purging again, and that's not what the goal is. To successfully recover from bulimia, you'll have to first change your perception of food.

Instead of looking at food as a necessary evil and keeping track of the calories, look at it as energy to do the things you love to do. Think about the things you would want to do if you had the energy to spare. Food is life; it enables you to do the things you want to in order to learn and improve your daily life. To fully live the life you want and deserve, you'll need to reframe how you see food.

Mindset on Food

Developing a healthy relationship with food is a difficult undertaking. It's a long, slow process that continues even after recovery. Nevertheless, there are still small moments and wins that can propel you into recovery, and it revolves around changing your mindset around food.

Food is not something to fear or be ashamed of. I know you've probably heard this before. As a source of external validation and someone who's been through it myself, I can tell you this as a fact. Once you realize that food isn't something to fear or look upon with shame or guilt, it's freeing. It's extremely difficult to change mindsets and focus instead on what you want to eat without that guilt.

Before you can shift your mindset around food, you must unlearn the lies you've been telling yourself. You're not fat, gross, or disgusting. You are beautiful, smart, and clever. You are worthy of kindness, appreciation, respect, and most importantly, love. The way you perceive yourself when you look in the mirror is not a reflection of who you are or what you're worth. Your worth isn't defined by a shell, but by what lies in your heart and mind.

Being skinny does not equate to being healthy. I'll say it again: Being skinny does not equate to being healthy. Shift your focus from obsessing over pudge and gaining weight, to being healthy! Love the body you're in and embrace its flaws and imperfections. Your body is the only one you have. The only solution to bulimia is to love the body you're in and heal from the pain that caused the disorder in the first place.

KEY TAKEAWAYS

Now that you've waded through this first chapter, I hope you've learned more about yourself and bulimia itself. This chapter contained a lot of information that is beneficial to your recovery. To summarize everything you've learned thus far, here is a list of the key takeaways from the chapter.

- Bulimia is a potentially life-threatening eating disorder that can have major repercussions later in life.
- Bulimia is eating then purging in ways such as extreme dieting and exercise, vomiting after eating, misusing laxatives, and more.
- The rate of eating disorders, especially bulimia nervosa, is more common in young women and teenage girls.
- It's common for sufferers of bulimia to also have mood disorders such as depression, anxiety, and bipolar disorder.
- Negative emotions especially cause the sufferer to purge because of intense feelings of guilt, shame, sadness, and anger.
- It feels like your life is not yours to control, but the one thing you can control is your diet. Bulimia is about the loss of control and grasping at something to gain a little control within your life.
- You're constantly analyzing your body and the food you consume by counting calories and purging when you're feeling low about yourself.
- This uncontrolled anxiety is impacting you and your ability to focus on school and function through daily activities.
- Heavy and light foods impact your body. Heavier foods sit in your stomach, which causes you to purge. Lighter foods are easily digested and therefore will make you purge less.
- Finding out what foods you can and cannot stomach will be beneficial to your recovery.

- Most importantly, please take care of your mind and body. You are not your weight and your perception about your weight. You're so much more.

You're now aware of the basics of bulimia and ways to implement strategies for your recovery. But is your eating disorder a crutch to living daily life? Find out in the next chapter.

2

THE CRUTCH

'*N*othing is more desirable than to be released from an affliction, but nothing is more frightening than to be divested of a crutch.' James Baldwin was a novelist whose career skyrocketed in the 1950s and 60s by challenging the status quo. The themes in his novels and essays provoke the reader's thoughts by revolving around the complexities of psychological and social pressures. Even though Baldwin's novels don't necessarily revolve around eating disorders, the quote refers to the crutches within the daily lives of his characters.

Similar to Baldwin's characters in his novels, most people rely on something in excess to cope with their feelings and daily life. Everyday existence can be stressful, and many utilize forms of entertainment as a way to cope and decompress from the day. However, crutches usually possess a negative connotation because they often refer to the overuse of unhealthy means of coping with life. Some people play video games, watch Netflix, or find other hobbies. On the other side of the spectrum, some abuse drugs and alcohol because of the inability to cope with trauma or other forms of emotional pain.

In a way, your eating disorder is your crutch to dealing with the pressures that come with daily life. Your anxiety and depression have skyrocketed due to several issues, and you're unsure of how to cope with them. What's worse is that either no one knows about your disorder or no one believes you. It's isolating and frightening to deal with this alone.

THE PRESSURES OF DAILY LIFE

The pressures of existing and being a fully-functional human being can be hard to bear. In between academic and social pressures, it's hard not to internalize that same pressure and harshly judge yourself for it. The cycle of emotional consumption and purging is your crutch, your only way to cope with the seemingly insurmountable pressures to exist as a person. Just because you're a teenager right now, your age range doesn't invalidate your fears and experiences. They are valid. Keeping up with the demand of pleasing your parents and friends while maintaining the perfection of society today is heavy to bear on someone so young. I'm here, and I care about how you're feeling. I've been through it as well, and I know exactly how you feel.

Emotional Consumption

When you're in a negative frame of mind, it's difficult to contain yourself when you feel the need to consume an excessive intake of calories. As a sufferer of bulimia, it's more common to eat sweeter, higher-caloric foods, and then purge them. According to a study by Annika P.C. Lutz et. al, 'The BN [bulimia nervosa] group showed an increased desire to eat high-calorie foods...' (2021). When you're feeling negative emotions, like your struggles with the expectations of daily activities, your impulse is to consume foods that promote a sugar high and a short-term feeling of positive emotions.

The struggles of living life with bulimia are exhausting on their own. Add academic and social struggles to the mix, and you create a messy situation as you try to combat and overcome your disorder.

Academic Struggles

With bulimia, it can feel like you're in a constant state of panic and feel inferior to your fellow students. You're not retaining the information you need to, and it's reflected in your grades. The eating disorder wiggles inside your brain and tells you that you're not smart because you cannot concentrate.

Some can still maintain academic success, but that doesn't necessarily mean they don't suffer as well. For example, I didn't struggle academically while suffering from bulimia. Instead, I focused primarily on my school work as a means to cope with my inability to talk about my feelings. When I did talk about them, I often was ignored, belittled, judged, or dismissed by those I was closest to. I may not have struggled with academics, but many often do.

You are not alone in your struggles with bulimia. In most cases in those who struggle with bulimia nervosa, this is an effect of the disorder. According to Jess P. Shatkin, MD, eating disorders such as bulimia '...interfere with interpersonal... and academic functioning..." (2020). In this context, it's understandable now that you cannot seem to concentrate as much on your academics.

With bulimia, you're lacking a lot of necessary nutrients and hydration to keep your brain functioning as well as it should be. Focus may be difficult to maintain because of the lack of nutrients and dehydration within the body. Due to the lack of vital nutrients and hydration, along with the brain chemistry that is associated with the disorder, it can feel like you're falling behind in classes. You may also be making more frequent bathroom trips upon arrival at school or following your lunch period. Those bathroom breaks could also be affecting your capability to be in the classroom. When you're absent from the classroom experience, you're also missing out on:

- Participation,
- Learning about the topics within each class,
- Writing effective notes,
- Asking important questions when the need arises, and
- Taking exams.

Being absent from school because of your disorder can also mean missing the entire day. If you're feeling especially sick, you'll talk to your parents about missing the day because you're feeling nauseous. It's not an entire lie, but it boils down to your most likely undiagnosed depression and anxiety. You've got so many other things in your life to worry about, and school sometimes needs to be on the back burner for now.

The onset of bulimia may not even be about your parents, but instead, you feel the need to escape the societal pressures and hierarchies at school.

Social Struggles

High school is rough for a lot of people. You're not alone in this feeling. The pretty and popular girls in your school are perfect. They have the right hairstyles, amazing makeup (if they need any at all), the perfect outfits and styles, and most importantly, they're skinny. A pang of envy shoots through you every time you see one of them. It feels like they were born lucky with amazing families and genetics. Meanwhile, you're sinking into the depths of despair and isolation.

In your mind, you harshly critique yourself in your weight and appearance. It's hard enough for you to concentrate on school as it is. Adding the anxiety and jealousy from seeing your peers in the classroom is another realm of hell in itself.

You have some friends at school, but no one you're particularly close to. Isolation is your only friend. You've probably been withdrawing from your friend group and not even realizing it. Either way, you're struggling with maintaining the friendships you once had or even struggling to make new ones. The balance you once had in keeping up with your friends and academics is now falling apart in front of you.

It's all because of the secret you've been keeping from your family and friends because you either don't want to worry them or you think they wouldn't believe you anyway. In your mind, the best way to ensure your eating disorder stays a secret is to alienate yourself from the rest of the world and close yourself inside it.

THE DIRTY LITTLE SECRET

The best-kept secret is the one that stays with you. You struggle silently with no one to listen to you about your problems and to validate you. No one offers their help because either you don't yet realize you have a problem, or you believe you need to figure this out by yourself. While figuring things out on your own is admirable, in the case of struggling with bulimia or any other mental health struggle, it is far better for your physical and mental health to ask for help. The secret that you bear weighs on you: the secret itself and the guilt that coincides with the secret-keeping. The dichotomy between keeping this aspect of your life hidden and wanting someone to uncover the truth remains ever-present in your mind.

Scheduling Your Purges

You've been dealing with this eating disorder, you may have a set schedule on a typical school day or the weekend. Discretion is key to preserving your secret. You might be scheduling when to purge for the appearance of a normal student without an eating disorder.

When I was in middle school, and throughout high school, I woke up each morning, dressed, drank a Slim Fast shake, and went to school. It held me over for a few hours, but the shake was the only thing I could stomach because it didn't feel heavy to me. While in school, I ate a Slim Fast bar. It felt light, so I never felt the need to purge while at school. When I came home, I snacked on junk food and then had dinner with my family. In my later years, as I struggled heavily with my disorder, I ate light meals, especially in restaurants.

After dinner with the family, I would purge in the shower sometimes. It wasn't all the time, but on the occasions where I felt overwhelmed, heavy, or depressed, I purged. For me, I turned on the shower and blared music as I purged to prevent my parents and sister from overhearing my purging.

For you, however, it may be different. You might have sched-uled your purges to maintain secrecy so your parents, friends, and teachers won't overhear you making yourself sick. Everyone's purge is different.

Because of the secrecy, there is a fear of who knows about your disorder, which then adds to your anxiety of facing your condition on your own.

Panic About Who Knows

No matter how much of a professional at hiding your secret from the world, you can still panic about who knows. There's a chance that someone will find out. It's a constant fear that only heightens when you're in the middle of a purge. While this never happened to me, it's still a nerve-racking experience. It creates more fear and therefore, self-imposed isolation. One of my experiences with a teacher disheartened me, leaving me with burning questions and still feeling panicky about who knows about my disorder.

I once attended a study session after school with my English teacher and a few friends. The teacher studied me and my appearance, then proceeded to tell me that there was a young girl in the school who was skinny like me, except that my face was rounder than the other girl's. She then continued to say that she and another teacher noticed that the girl was getting thinner and thinner, suspecting that an eating disorder may be at play.

I was shocked. I simply stared at her, thinking about how this girl is silently killing herself. My teacher and her coworker were observing it from afar instead of stepping in for some intervention or other form of help. Even though the problem was obvious, just like mine was, no adult had stepped up to get the other student the help she desperately needed. Just because someone finds out, it doesn't necessarily mean that they will help you. It plays into the other fear that contradicts bulimia at its core: What if no one finds out?

Panic of Not Being Discovered

On the other end of the spectrum of your complex emotions, there is always a fear of not being discovered. The previous statement contradicts the fear of discovery in the first place; it's the reason why you're trying to hide your deep suffering from bulimia.

You know you need help, but perhaps you're not ready to completely accept it yet. Maybe you want to be found out. Maybe, instead of a schedule, you've made it easier for someone to discover your secret. All of this erodes your self-worth because it validates your deepest fear that no one cares about you. It's a fear we all face in our lives. Especially with those of us who have struggled in silence with our eating disorders, it's difficult to admit to someone you love that you're struggling with the perception of your body and mental health issues.

The little voice in the back of your head is screaming for help, but none has come. The same little voice also reminds you that if someone truly loved and cared about you, they would check on you. They would confront you. They would do *something* to help you and make you realize you're not alone, and that you have their support.

Because of the complexities of your fears, it creates a vicious cycle of emotions that are constantly at war. You want your secret concealed, but you also want someone to uncover the lies and deceit and guide you to receive the help you need.

The Rapid Cycle of Emotions

This rapid cycle of absolute panic no matter the outcome is your reality for the duration of your disorder. The juxtaposition of both of these fears is difficult to understand and even more so to deal with. The logic behind the fears, to a person who doesn't have an eating disorder, can appear to not make any sense. That's the problem with bulimia, though. It relies on and feeds on your negative emotions. Emotions are complicated, and so are the people who experience them.

The fear of discovery of your struggle with bulimia competes with the need to feel seen and heard. It's a daily battle that plays over and over in your head even when you're not purging. You've mastered your secret so well that it's hard for anyone to truly help you. The excuses and lies have become all too convincing.

DEAD WEIGHT, SECRET PROBLEMS

You're carrying the weight of your disorder without anyone currently knowing about it. It's a secret problem, and you have no one to discuss your problems with. You're completely isolated from everyone and have even withdrawn from the things you once cared about and loved to do. This is also your depression wedging itself into your daily activities.

The prolonged bathroom visits are the norm for you and those you surround yourself with. Carrying this dead weight is one of the immediate reasons for your long stints in the bathroom. It's also your crutch for not being present in class and being around those who are the objects of your envy. It makes it easier to cope with your academic struggles. The only solution you have come up with to the problems you are currently facing is to hold them inside and keep a secret, then purge them out and allow yourself to feel the swirl of emotions when you're alone.

Coping With Life Through Excess

Bulimia heightens your appetite followed by the cruel need to purge the food you just ate. The food, just like your mind, is unsettled. The only peace you can kind of feel is after the cycle of eating and purging.

Consumption of food and then purging it is how you cope with the stresses in your life. It feels as though it's the only way you can control how you feel without those who love you asking questions. For a moment the world seems manageable when you eat. You're fine with your existence, and then hate yourself when you realize how many calories you have just consumed. The waves of nausea accompanied by the dizziness in your head then lead you straight to the bathroom.

The secret you're holding inside is also causing immense amounts of both embarrassment and guilt. You know that what you're doing is unhealthy, but it's the only way you can deal with the swirling negative emotions compounded with social and academic pressures. As you're inducing yourself to vomit or other extreme ways to purge, you feel the heat of embarrassment and the cold, dead weight of guilt creep inside your mind.

Embarrassment

One of the reasons you hide your eating disorder is because of the embarrassment you feel over the inability to keep down the food you've eaten. You know that your parents work hard to keep the food on the table, so to speak, but you're embarrassed and ashamed you can't keep it down. It does not matter how hard you try; your body and mind succumb to the need to purge.

There's also the embarrassment that comes from potential discovery. Currently, there still is a stigma against eating disorders in the minds of the ignorant. You don't want to have your disorder mocked in front of you or behind your back. Rumor mills in high school spread like a disease and infect the minds of the faculty and students. You'll become even more paranoid and afraid if your secret is exposed. The kids your age right now are cruel, and that cruelty will open the floodgates to a harder recovery if someone were to find out about your secret.

The embarrassment of struggling to maintain your weight and everyone in your school knowing about it would be too much stress and anxiety for you. What would be just as humiliating is if you found out that no one cared enough about you to ask if something is wrong. You would lie, of course, but their persistence would mean that they do want the best for you. But what if no one even notices your struggle? It must be a sign that they don't care about you as much as you originally thought.

Embarrassment is one of the reasons your eating disorder must remain a secret. The humiliation and shame you feel constantly weigh on your psyche. It's another dead weight that must be purged. The same is true for guilt.

Guilt

While it was briefly discussed in Chapter 1, guilt is an extremely complex emotion that is triggered by intense feelings of wrongdoings. In the last chapter, the concept of guilt was explored mainly in respect to the act of eating and purging the food you just consumed. The guilt revolving around bulimia and its implications of not being able to finish the food you were given causes you to feel guilty like you've done something wrong. The physical aspect of guilt in the disorder weighs on you.

In this chapter, however, guilt references the secret-keeping of your disorder. Keeping secrets and telling outright lies causes a majority of people to feel guilty. In your struggle with bulimia, it's normal to feel remorse over keeping your eating disorder a secret. You have myriad reasons for concealing this part of your life from others that are personal to you. No matter the reason, there is still the heaviness of regret and sadness that accompanies your guilt.

Guilt also has its physical side effects when prolonged such as heightened feelings of anxiety. Anxiety fuels the nausea you endure daily; your stomach is tied in knots as you realize you are deliberately keeping your disorder from the people you love. Deceit wedges itself in between yourself and those closest to you. The guilt you're feeling is an effect of the rift you are unconsciously making by choosing to keep your eating disorder hidden.

Remorse racks through your body and soul with each lie you tell to cover up your struggle with bulimia. When you give excuses to your friends for using the restroom as frequently as you do, especially if the need to purge hits you more than once, you're intentionally lying to your friends. The immediate result is to feel guilty for not trusting your friends with the truth but also lying to preserve your secret.

To begin the recovery process, you must learn to trust those you know love you. The people who are closest to you vary as everyone's situation is unique, but to start with, open up to someone about your struggles with bulimia. I know it's such a frightening thing to do. But I can promise you, it will be worth it.

KEY TAKEAWAYS

As we end the chapter, take a moment to reflect on the things you have learned about bulimia thus far. Have you learned more about yourself and realized that your disorder is your way of coping with the hardships in your life? Through academic and social struggles, on top of trying to overcome this disorder on your own, your life has been hard to wade through. Because of all the information that was in this chapter, allow me to help you to unpack by listing the key points.

- Crutches are used by many people to combat the crippling exhaustion and despair that can lead them down undesirable paths.
- Bulimia is your crutch to cope with academic and social pressures imposed by the school, society, and your parents through emotional consumption.
- Because of your swirling negative emotions, causes you to emotionally consume an excess of food, then purge it as a means of coping with these negative emotions.
- You probably struggle with academic hardships. It can be harder to focus on your schoolwork because of the lack of attendance in the classroom.
- Another reason you may struggle academically is that your brain is lacking the nutrients and hydration it needs to fully process information and keep your attention focused.
- In addition to academic struggles in school, there are also social struggles as well. You are keeping a secret from your friends; consequently, you are starting to withdraw from them.

- Because of this secret, you have found ways to keep it hidden from people to not rouse any suspicion of your struggle.
- You may schedule your purges following a schedule to protect your secret from discovery.
- You're in a constant panic over who knows or who could potentially know. Subsequently, you hide your disorder to save face. The reasons are yours, but some examples are to prevent bullying or being frowned upon.
- You're also in a state of panic over what would happen if someone found out. This fear increases your anxiety and self-imposed isolation. However, even if someone does find out, there's a chance they might not help you.
- There is also the deeply rooted fear of no one noticing your disorder, and therefore you realize no one cares about you and you have no support system. No one catching you and talking to you about it further erodes your self-esteem.
- The rapid cycling of emotions of both keeping your secret and allowing yourself to be caught in its contradictory hell.
- Because you're carrying a harmful secret, it becomes a dead weight both in your stomach and inside your mind. It's a weight that is difficult to bear on your own.
- The secret to your eating disorder is how you cope with external stressors; the only way is to repeat the cycle of excessive food intake and the cruel need to purge it immediately after.
- The brain is initially wired to decrease appetite under major distress, but sufferers of bulimia have the opposite effect followed by purging.

- The embarrassment of keeping the secret, of the purging itself, and of being caught are all a part of the rapid cycling thoughts as you purge. You don't want to become part of the high school rumor mill, but you also know it's embarrassing to admit that you have a problem.
- Guilt manifests in many forms. In this chapter specifically, it's the guilt of the secret itself that's weighing you down and creating a rift between yourself and the ones you love.

After reading this chapter, you should be more self-aware about how you perceive yourself as well as how much of your eating disorder is truly a secret. A culmination of daily living and the struggles of simply existing can truly be an insurmountable mountain. This chapter mainly focused on school and how you're able to hide it while attending, but what about at home? The next chapter will focus solely on the relationship dynamic between yourself and your parents.

3

FAMILY RELATIONSHIPS

*T*ake a second to reflect on the relationship you have with your parents and siblings (if you have any). Is there never a quiet moment in the house because of constant conflict between the family? Maybe your parents don't give you the space you need to talk and invalidate you at every turn. Or perhaps your older and younger siblings' relentless comments about your weight have become worse.

In most cases of bulimia, the problems first arise within the systemic rules and responsibilities of each family member. The role each member takes is how you then perceive the outside world. Because you're on one of the lowest tiers in the family system regarding importance and power, you're an easy target for comments, abuse, and manipulation among family members.

It's crucial to learn about the systems within your family to find your dynamic of power. Once you learn and understand the role you play within your family, it will be easier to understand how to maneuver past those unseen boundaries.

The problem is, you don't have a space where you feel safe and heard, except perhaps your room where you're not bothered as much. Your room is your safe space.

What you're most likely experiencing right now is trauma at the hands of your family, and all parties may not even realize it.

FAMILY TRAUMA

Trauma is either experiencing or seeing a disturbing event or series of events happening within a short frame of time. A lot of times, this is a sudden moment in time that results in bodily harm or even a loss of life. According to apa.org, some of these instances are:

- A car accident,
- Physical and emotional abuse,
- Losing a loved one suddenly,
- Environmental disasters, or
- A divorce (Accessed 2022).

The same event also causes a shift in the observer's mindset about what is considered safe. Their previous frame of safety in life has been completely shattered in one singular event. It can be summed up in a simple sentence that is both horrifying and chilling.

'My world is no longer safe.'

The problem with trauma is that it often can go unnoticed for long periods of time, as the sufferers' previous concept of the world is completely broken. Emotions are suppressed to fit into society and not admit the experience that they had was real. Or worse, if they do talk about the experience, in the cases of abuse and neglect, no one believes them.

For those who suffer from bulimia, trauma in the family is a major factor in the development of an eating disorder. In some cases of bulimia patients, there are underlying abusive relationships between the parental figures and the child.

The Father

When looking at the parents of bulimia and the parent-daughter relationship, studies have shown that the father is the first culprit behind the trauma within the family. Many young women and adolescent children described their relationship with their fathers as tense, cold, and distanced from them. However, in the cases of abuse, it can lead to complex trauma and control.

Complex trauma and abuse in teenage girls stem from their relationship with their fathers in most cases. According to a study from A.J. Saunokonoko, 'Fathers of daughters with BN [bulimia nervosa] were found to be a source of fear, control, abuse, emotional and physical avoidance and gender diminishment' (2022). The fathers of teenage girls with bulimia are often controlling and abusive, especially with comments about their weight. Keep in mind, however, that the mothers can also be responsible for unrealistic expectations and body-shaming to the point of incurring bulimia.

Because of this overbearing control and fear, the dysfunctional perception of the parents of teenage girls and young women paves the way for this disorder often accompanied by a barrage of mood disorders. This skewed and untrue perception is how young adolescent girls such as yourself will view their bodies and their self-image.

My father wasn't necessarily controlling, but he had high expectations of me. He and I never spoke of the disorder itself. However, he still made comments to me about my weight. Every so often he pointed out how thin I was. He called me a bone rack at dinner on one occasion. When I told him not to call me that, he laughed and did it again. Due to his blatant disregard for my feelings in those moments, I felt as though I couldn't trust him and tell him about what was going on with me, hiding under the surface.

My father also made me uncomfortable in restaurants. For years, my father ordered something similar to mine when we went out to eat. It made me uncomfortable. He switched chairs during family events at restaurants if we were on the same side so he could sit opposite me and watch me from the opposing side of the table instead. It felt like a fishbowl. He thought he was being funny, but instead, I felt overwatched and constantly scrutinized. My cousin attempted to speak to me about my disorder and voiced concern over how I only ate salads at dinner and how thin I was. Even still, I didn't feel like I could open up about anything.

The aspect of control can lead to a lack of identity and perfection among those who suffer from bulimia. While the relationship between your father and yourself may be tense, so may also be the relationship with your mother.

The Mother

The mother also has a huge impact and responsibility in raising their child. Oftentimes in society, the role of care-taker rests on the mother's shoulders. However, the same responsibility is faulty at best in the case of those who suffer from bulimia.

In addition to the control of the father, patients with bulimia also record the hostility they have towards their mothers. According to a study conducted by Xiaorong Zhou, the '...conflictual theme of the mother-daughter relationship can be summarized as, the weakness and anxiety of the mother... limit[s] their capability to support and love their daughter' (2019).

The control can be based on bending to beauty standards, such as forcing the daughter to exercise at an unhealthy level or even expressing their disapproval of the weight she has seemingly gained. The constant barrage of comments made and the control over the lives of those with bulimia breeds contempt and low self-image.

The same study from Zhou also suggests the participants of the study only want one underlying feeling. All they want to feel is that they are loved by their mother and father. This need to feel loved is a universal need for all humans; without it, we are doomed to a life of isolation.

At such a vulnerable age while you're developing into an adult, it can be brutal navigation to unlearn the behaviors you utilized to survive. Your parents are of no help; it is almost impossible for them to see your value as a unique person and not as a miniature version of themselves.

My mother wasn't controlling, but she didn't have the time for me. She was often absent in my upbringing. My mother was working towards her Ph.D. during my middle and high school years. In between working at the university itself while attending classes and working on her dissertations, she had little time to contend with my eating disorder. Her absence was one of the reasons why I felt so alone in my struggles.

The Siblings

Siblings are arguably one of the most underrated values in how a person adapts and develops into adulthood. Based on the formative years of adolescence into adulthood, siblings tend to develop a closer bond with the individual than even the parents. While not much is understood concerning siblings and bulimia, there still can be trauma there as well. The siblings don't have to necessarily be blood-related. With the influx of blended families, they can range from full siblings to step-siblings and even adopted siblings. Each family is unique with its variety of communication and support.

Having at least one sibling in your family can offer the support you need that your parents cannot give you. The relationship between yourself and each sibling can either be a supportive one or one full of conflict. If you're experiencing trauma, neglect, and abuse, chances are your sibling is feeling the same.

However, some parents may favor the prodigy over the average. Some may even pit the siblings against each other to establish the dominant role between themselves and their siblings, regardless of age. While this may be an extreme representation of abuse, some family systems engage in this behavior.

Depending on the relationship you have with your sibling(s), if you have any, you may have confided your secret in them, if you have a good relationship with them built on trust and shared experiences. Or, you don't have a good relationship with them and you're keeping your secret from them because you don't trust them.

My sister had a hit-or-miss mentality when it came to me. If someone alerted her to the fact that I wasn't eating lunch, she confronted me at home. She never included my parents when she confronted me, so it was just the two of us. However, her tone and the way she yelled at me obviously didn't make her a safe person to go to for emotional struggles. When it came to bulimia, she, along with the rest of my family, had no idea. They just knew I was spending a great deal of time in the bathroom.

As I was standing in the door frame of the bathroom, my sister caught me and remarked in front of my mother, 'Look at her, Mom, she's so skinny she looks like a toothpick in the door frame.' I said nothing and neither did my mom. I had no support from my family no matter which way I turned.

The family systems that are in place in your household represent the power of each person. Because each system differs from the next, it's also not surprising if your family has created an environment where your eating disorder is allowed to form and exist. For me, the result was that my waistline shrank and my hip bones were present.

FAMILY SYSTEMS AND BULIMIA

The dynamic of your family is one of the major causes of your development of bulimia. Dealing with family is a difficult experience because of the varying personalities within the systems. If one family member is considered the black sheep, or the one who appears to be the most troubled or odd, they can be ostracized from the home and ignored or isolated.

Think for a moment about the relationships with each of your parents. How do they show affection (if they do at all) and how do they punish you? Neglect and abuse are also common occurrences for a young teenage girl to experience trauma. Consequently, teenage girls such as yourself develop bulimia to cope with living in your home.

Parenting Styles: Authoritative, Permissive, and Authoritarian

There are three types of parenting styles: authoritarian, permissive, and authoritative. Each parenting style is based on the personality of the parent and a result of how they were parented. It's a cycle that can be broken through active steps and recognizing their faults as a parent. Each parenting style has its consequences for correcting the behavior of the child(ren) in question. Just because one parent has a specific style, it doesn't mean that the other parent mirrors them. Instead, it could be the opposite. However, some parental childrearing is harsher than others.

The authoritarian parenting style may be the one you're currently experiencing with your parents. This style refers to childrearing without a care for the child's feelings or the ability to express themselves. It's often associated with a cold, lack of nurturing personality with harsh punishments for the parent to maintain control. According to Tiago Santos et. al, 'Parents exerting psychological control are described as being primarily focused on their own psycho-logical and emotional issues and their authority role as parent' (2018). The controlling behavior and rigid bound-aries allow the child to have relatively little freedom and the ability to express themselves in a healthy manner.

On the opposite side, the permissive parenting style allows children to have complete control over themselves. Parents with this style don't exert any type of boundaries and allow the child free reign. They also don't employ methods of punishment. This is essentially the hands-off method, allowing the children to regulate their impulses and desires. In some cases, the child believes that the parent doesn't truly care for them because there is no stability or foundation to build upon as an adult.

The last parenting style is the authoritative style, where there is open two-way communication between the parent and the child. This style is considered to be the best style according to developmental psychologists who have studied the long-term effects of this particular choice in childrearing. The parents utilize punishments by setting firm boundaries for the child not to cross. The punishments are less severe compared to the authoritarian style and are conveyed through open communication and accountability for both the child and the parents. There is warmth and nurturing present in this type of childrearing.

My parents were mainly authoritarian, controlling every aspect of my life. My mother was mostly absent, but she still had her say in my life. My parents controlled my major, what classes I took, what college I was going to attend, and everything else in my life that would look good on a college resume. This was especially during my high school years.

My high school boyfriend was my means of escape and relaxation. Each day I was meant to call when I get somewhere and call when I leave. If I didn't call when I arrived and left, I received a lecture when I returned home for the evening. Food was never truly mentioned. It didn't matter what I ate during the day because, according to my mother, I was eating a full dinner with the family at night.

My father would check on both me and my sister each night to ensure we were sleeping well. He doesn't sleep well, so he would often get up at odd hours of the night to check on us. If I only ate salads at dinners out with my family, he would comment positively on it saying he was going to try and start eating more healthy like me and try more salads. He did love my sister and me, but there were facets of his personality and his unwavering stare at dinner often made me uncomfortable.

What type of parenting techniques do your parents use? Reflect for a moment on whether you feel valued and heard when discussing a problem with your parents and how they respond to you. Do you feel unheard and unseen?

Although the blanket statement for parents is that they want the best for their children, sometimes the pressures they place on those children are unrealistic and unattainable. For many with a certain type of parenting style, this causes the child's need to feel perfect to gain the love and acceptance they crave from their parents.

Perfection and Bulimia

Most often in authoritarian parenting styles, there is an inherent emphasis on perfection. Perfection in itself is not necessarily bad; it can lead to great things if implemented at a time when necessary. However, it's the dysfunctional need to be perfect at everything to gain acceptance from your parents that can be a problem. When you are criticized in an unhealthy manner, it leads to low self-esteem and internalizing the pain associated with the criticism.

When children don't meet the expectations set by their parents, it leads to the child internalizing this failure. Santos et. al writes about this issue, 'The failure on such accomplishment would set off a stable pattern of parental criticism and guilt induction....' This would create '...children prone to negative self-evaluations in contexts where they would not be able to meet such external and self-imposed standards' (2018).

During my senior year of high school, I came home some days to my father on the phone with the college admission office asking for an update on my admission status. I dreaded the day the official rejection letter came. We had a family meeting on the next steps, and I felt like such a failure. I had been accepted to three other universities, but we didn't talk about them when those acceptance letters came because the one they were waiting for didn't arrive. This was the university they wanted me to attend, and this setback made such a lasting impression on me as a failure.

Because your parents are so in tune with perfection, it causes you to internalize these feelings. Since you are unable to fully meet the expectations and perfection of your family, you are forced to look inward at yourself and hyperfixate on the things that are wrong with you such as your weight.

This lack of two-way communication with your parents overlaps with every facet of living and dealing with your parents every day. In the case of sitting with your parents at the dinner table, that lack of communication reflects at the heart of where family discussion and bonding should happen.

THE TROUBLE WITH FAMILY DINNERS

Throughout my middle school and high school career, as I suffered from bulimia, I still sat down at the dinner table with my family. I picked at the food in front of me, my nausea weighing me down. I knew that I had to push through dinner to go into the bathroom and purge. My family and I rarely discussed my weight unless to poke fun at me for how thin I was.

Family dinners are usually the time and place where parents check in with their children and vice versa. It's the place where families come together and talk about their day and decompress from the notion of experiencing everyday life.

In families that have someone suffering from bulimia, it's a time and place that is often the reason for more dread. On top of academic and social struggles, sufferers of bulimia trudge to the dinner table and refrain from as much conversation as possible.

Paradoxically, the dinner table is where the intimacy and bonding of the family happen, and it's also a source of food and sharing of food. While a difficult situation to maneuver, it's also a source of dependability and stability within the household. It's predictable from the conversation and sharing of food and stories to even the placement of everyone who sits at the table with you.

Isolation From Conversation

You're sitting at the dinner table with your parents and siblings. Your parents are opposite of each other at the ends of the table, while you and your siblings are smushed in the middle. This placement of each parent and sibling reflects the balance of power within the household: the parents make the decisions and the children are stuck in the middle with little to no say about their lives. The conversation often revolves around the day, what accomplishments you made, and the expectations for your collective futures. From an outsider's perspective, it may seem like a normal, healthy relationship. Unfortunately, the appearances don't last.

The conversations around the table are about you, but often-times they don't involve you. Before you can insert your thoughts on a subject, the conversation shifts. You're left isolated from the talk of the table. Or worse, they speak as though you're not there. They speak about you in the third person, as if you're incapable of making your own decisions. In my experience, my family talked about me but refused to include me in the conversation itself.

It's Never 'How Are You Doing'

Your family is so focused on your academic achievements that there is no room to ask you how you're doing. Family dinners tend to revolve around the grades and future expec-tations set by your parents for appearances of perfection. To them, you're not given too much to handle; you can easily adapt to the new expectations because they did it when they were your age. Why shouldn't you be able to handle it too?

The only focus at the dinner table is how you're excelling academically. Even if you are excelling in several subjects, they still find a way to bring you down. They never ask you how you're doing emotionally; all they seem to care about is your schooling so that you can further your education. Furthering your education and controlling your major in a field you don't necessarily want is the trajectory they have planned for you.

Lack of Communication

When you do open up to them about some of the struggles you're facing, academically or otherwise, the only thing your parents bring to the metaphorical table is to point out exactly where you're going wrong. The constant critiquing is exhausting. You look forward to the moment you can purge to expel the weight from both the meal and your parents' expectations.

Any attempts to speak about your struggle with mental health and your eating disorder are met with eye rolls, sighing, and then abruptly ending the conversation. You've tried to talk to both of your parents separately and together, but the attempts were made in vain. They simply won't acknowledge your issues, therefore giving you another reason to purge.

The problem with my family is that no one wanted to listen to me. I tried to talk to my family about it, but they essentially gaslit me and told me that I just simply didn't eat. When talking to my sister about my eating disorder, she rolled her eyes and reassured me that no, it wasn't an eating disorder. Then she walked away from me. I never discussed it with my father or my mother. We never talked about it, adding to the isolation I felt within my family.

Comments About Weight

My family never really mentioned my appearance or my weight that often. The closest we ever came to talking about it was when my family and I were at one of the high school football games. A fellow mother of one of the cheerleaders mentioned to my mother that I was looking a little thin. Later that week, my mother asked me if I was trying to lose weight. I lied and told her that no, I wasn't trying to lose weight. The conversation was dropped afterward, except to ask me why I would spend so much time in the bathroom.

However, this may not be your experience. As you sit at the dinner table, minding your own business, out of left field one of your siblings decides it would be hysterical if they started to make jokes about your weight. They point out the puffiness of your face. Your parents join in and joke about how much weight you've been gaining lately because of your immense love of food. Everyone at the table collectively laughs at your expense. They know it's one of your pain points, and to be cruel, they throw it back in your face. Your family doesn't hold back on the punches and verbal abuse they give you.

The cruelty at the dinner table is only one of the common places where your family lands hard on the jokes of your puffy face or the rolls of fat on your belly as you sit down. The dead weight of mockery has left you feeling nauseous. You want to purge right now, but you know you'll have to wait until after dinner and dessert.

What your parents and siblings don't know is that their enduring comments and jokes about the little bit of weight you've gained or lost are hurting you. The permanent effect of these comments and conversations is now your reality: your eating disorder bulimia.

The meal is over, but the dessert is in front of you. You gorge on the food despite the ever-increasing weight in your belly. It gives you a moment of reprieve.

Knowing your family is about to make a snarky comment to you, you ignore them and run to the bathroom without another word. As you walk away, you hear your father make one more scathing remark about your weight before shutting yourself in the bathroom for a while.

Finally, you're able to purge.

COMPLICATED EMOTIONS

As you sit in front of the porcelain deity, you reflect on the conversation at dinner. Your skull is so full of struggling through the day, that it feels as though it's tearing you apart. Or, at least your stomach feels as though it's been through a shredder, and the only solution is to purge the contents of your meal.

From shame and humiliation to isolation and loneliness, you're feeling so many negative emotions as your stomach heaves repeatedly. You've grown quiet with your purges; you barely make a sound as you empty the feelings you have left. Or, maybe you have another sound barrier to drown out the noises of your purge.

The comments about your weight are the first to go. After all, it's not like you hate the taste of food or even dread it when it enters your system. Just the opposite. You love food, or used to, before the onset of your disorder. It's the over-whelming amount of remarks about weight made by the family who is supposed to be your support system. The immense fear of becoming fat—or worse, obese—is one that they nitpick and use as a weapon against you. Because of this intense fear, that's next to be removed from your system through purging.

Short-Lived Happiness

Once you're through, you brush your teeth carefully and rinse with mouthwash. No one knows about your disorder; they won't even be able to tell you purged because of the mouthwash and toothpaste combined.

For a fleeting expression of time, you're happy that the weight has been lifted. The reprieve from the comments and the day lightened your mood. Before falling asleep, your mind drifts from the happiness of the weight lifted to the crushing despair you feel now.

Loneliness Within the Family

When the world is still, that's often when the daily events play in your mind. The numerous dinner conversations about you but not involving you interrupts your ability to fall asleep. Underneath the agony of living another day at school and home, one crucial fact remains with you.

No one listens to you or your feelings. You don't want your family to know about your eating disorder, but paradoxically, you just want them to care about you and how you feel. You don't want them to obsess over your academics and your lack of accomplishments. You just want to feel accepted and loved for who you are right now, not the potential your parents think you have.

Everyone in your family simply negates any expression of emotion by rerouting the conversation or completely stopping it in its tracks. Because of this, your loneliness has made it easier to choose the option of isolation.

Self-Imposed Isolation

Since no one in your household listens to you anyway, the best option is to completely isolate yourself and pretend you don't exist in the same space as them. Your siblings are thriving, at least so it seems, and you're the only one who is stuck in the realm of depression and eating disorders. In your mind, no one in your family deserves to know about your struggle with bulimia if they can't even be bothered to ask how you're doing.

The only role you play in your family is to be the butt of everyone's jokes, including your parents. The patterns of gaslighting and outright callousness toward you are beyond repair. You've tried your best at communicating with them that you're struggling with an eating disorder that's spiraled out of control. Anger at your situation and your family surges through you. But mostly, you're just disappointed in yourself.

Disappointment in Yourself

Disappointment and guilt often walk hand-in-hand. You don't want to tell your family about your disorder, but you also want them to figure it out. The disappointment in yourself festers in multiple ways such as:

- Not being able to stand up for yourself to your family about the weight comments,
- Not being able to tell them about your constant daily battle with bulimia,
- Not being able to fully control your eating and purging habits,
- Being unable to contend with the fact your siblings are perfect in the minds of your parents,
- The inability to keep food down even if you want to, and
- Obsessing over your weight even when you know it's unhealthy.

I'm sure you can come up with more examples than this as reasons behind the disappointment in yourself. In all these instances, you're upset over the things you can't control. You feel like a failure in every aspect of your life, and there's nothing you can do about it because of the lacking support system you have in your family.

I'm here to remind you that you're not a failure. You have value and merit outside of your weight and your relationship with your family. The emotions swirling around your brain as a result of your family don't have to define you. You're valid for feeling the way you do. You're allowed to express the emotions you bottle up inside because you think no one cares about you. But I care about you and your future. Bottling up these emotions only allows them to fester. They won't disappear like you want them to.

KEY TAKEAWAYS

This chapter I'm sure was a hard one to digest. From the discussion of trauma and abuse in the family to discussing the conversations around the family table, a lot of information was pushed onto you. It's time now to walk through some of the key takeaways of this chapter.

- The onset of bulimia can be caused by the family itself.
- For some survivors of trauma, bulimia is a way to cope with the instances of abuse and neglect at the hands of the parents themselves and/or through the cruelty of siblings.
- Family systems and the functioning of each member of the family can be seen through the family system itself.
- There are three types of parenting styles: authoritarian, permissive, and authoritative. Most parents of teenagers suffering from bulimia fall into the category of authoritarian because of the overwhelming amount of control the parent has, along with harsh punishments.

- Perfection and bulimia often coincide: the parents place immense pressure on the accomplishments and performances of their children, resulting in the need to internalize that perfection to maintain the sufferer's appearance and weight.
- While family dinners are often the space for intimate conversations between the family, it can result in the slow withdrawal of the teenager with bulimia.
- Because of this withdrawal, the sufferers tend to isolate themselves from conversations because they don't possess the autonomy to speak about themselves and their struggles.
- The conversation often revolves around performance in school and rarely does the discussion venture into how the children are coping with life. If this happens, the conversation quickly moves to another subject.
- This lack of communication will create resentment from the sufferer of bulimia because of the inability of the parents to discuss the struggle of their children.
- The off-handed insults and comments about weight, while made in a joking manner, cause eating disorders such as bulimia.
- The complicated emotions surrounding the family in the mind of the sufferer are paradoxical. They want to talk about their struggle, but they know their parents will be unable to fully handle it.
- The only happiness the teenagers suffering from bulimia feel is short-lived when they purge out the contents of their stomachs from the interaction with their families.
- The numerous negative interactions between the teenager and the rest of the family cause loneliness

within the family system, and therefore many sufferers experience self-isolation.

- The constant barrage of negativity often leaves the sufferer disappointed in themselves and their lives. They often compare themselves to their parents or siblings and wonder what's wrong with them.

Now that you've finished this chapter, I hope you're feeling more aware of the systems surrounding your family. This chapter was a heavy one, but a necessary one to fully express the impact of how your family affects the severity and status of your struggle with bulimia. In the next chapter, we'll dive into the social aspect of dealing with bulimia, including social media and its influences.

4

ELEPHANT IN THE ROOM,
ELEPHANT IN THE STOMACH

'*L*ook at this roll in my stomach! I'm fat!' Your best friend shows you her protruding stomach over her waistline in the bathroom before your first class together. In mock horror, you tell her there's nothing there, and that she looks beautiful today. Her skin, hair, and makeup are flawless; she could have easily been mistaken for the goddess Aphrodite. She scoffs at your attempt to ease her mind, then she prattles about the number of boys she's texting. You roll your eyes, but laugh at the insanity her life is. Deep down, though, you want that kind of attention and external validation from admiring boys in your grade or higher.

You constantly validate your friends whenever they need your support: academics, high school romance, and even the frequent fight between them and their parents. Your home-life is decent; every now and again you'll get into an argument with your parents, but it's nothing like some of the other kids in your class. Sure, your parents might not listen to you most of the time, but it's something you can deal with.

They're not as bad as they could be, and your friends know that too. They consider your parents the 'cool' parents, and your house is typically the hangout spot.

You see the beauty in everyone but yourself. If only you could somehow change.

Enter bulimia. Everyone's bodies are changing, and somehow you've gained some weight. You once were proud of your skinniness, but now it's different. You used to be the one the boys chased at recess, but now barely anyone looks at you. So you go on TikTok and look up some makeup tutorials. All the influencers on there are so pretty and, most importantly, skinny. To combat your weight gain, you start to purge.

IGNORING THE PROBLEM

You've been eating and then purging your stomach for a while now. Your friends have noticed something is wrong, but they typically don't speak up. If they do, you just tell them you've been drinking a lot of water and are constantly going to the bathroom. You shake your trusty water bottle in your hand, cementing the idea that you're going to relieve yourself. They think nothing of it. What they don't know is that you're relieving yourself differently.

As much as your friends want to help you, they instead ignore the problem by pretending it doesn't exist. They've noticed the changes in your demeanor and how you perceive yourself and the world around you. Either they don't know how to confront you about the problem or if it's just another phase you're embracing.

Frequent Visitations to the Restroom

After a while, your friends have now become suspicious of your behavior. There is a problem with you; that much is obvious, but they don't know what the problem is. You still want to keep your secret to yourself, so you don't tell them.

They do notice, however, the frequent visits to the restroom during classes and right before your lunch period ends. And you're in there for a while. The problem is becoming more and more obvious to them, and you.

Constant Hydration and Newfound Love for Healthy Food

In addition to the frequent restroom visits, they also notice your intake of water has increased. Before, you hated water because it was so flat and tasteless. Now, they have come to realize this change in pace must mean that something more sinister is boiling under the surface. Your friends initially chalk it up to you wanting to stay hydrated for healthy reasons. But your diet has changed too. Instead of the big meals you used to buy at the school cafeteria, you're now packing salads you begged your parents for. Little did anyone know, it was the only thing you can keep in your stomach.

They noticed your harsh judgment on the foods they've been eating as well. Before you'd eat the same things they did, but now you're relaying the calorie intake of the brownies they used to enjoy, along with everything else. This drastic shift into a healthy mindset isn't like you normally.

Slowly, you begin to withdraw yourself from your friend group. With the gradual obsession over your weight now that your bulimia is in full swing, it's difficult for you to be around them.

Withdrawals From the Friend Group

Because of your eating disorder, you begin to remove yourself from social situations. At first, it was a party here and there you didn't necessarily want to attend. As time passed and your eating disorder grew more severe, you knew it would be more of an obstacle to hide your eating disorder due to the frequent restroom breaks after eating. Socialization outside of school is a burden you don't want or need right now. Any discoveries made by your friends would result in shame and humiliation from your friend group.

A few of your friends have made the attempt to ask you what's wrong, but you shrug it off and say you're fine. They don't think you'd lie to them, so they continue to believe that there isn't anything wrong and you're implementing a new phase in your life.

As a result, your friends completely ignore you, purposefully oblivious to your problems and your struggle with bulimia.

THE INFLUENCE OF YOUR FRIENDS

In a lot of cases, however, sufferers of bulimia don't necessarily have these kinds of friendships in high school. Instead, they are all friendships based on situational and geographic locations; once you have graduated and moved forward, you'll find that most of the 'friends' you have only served a minor purpose in your life.

Think for a moment about the friends you currently have. Are they supportive and try to help you? Or, do they tend to ignore you, furthering your isolation? Think about the environment that your friends have created and the conversations they have. What are those conversations about?

Hard Truths

In 2013, a study was conducted in Canada that was based on how young girls who suffered from bulimia felt about their friendships. According to Laurissa Fauchoux, the conductor of the study, 'Friendships influence adolescent girls' self-esteem, body image, dieting, body dissatisfaction, and eating disorder symptoms, through bullying and peer teasing, appearance conversations, and group dieting' (2013). Your friends may be one of the reasons you have developed bulimia with the constant discussions of pointing out body weight and your appearance.

High school can be a grueling experience, especially if you have an eating disorder. The constant pressure to look perfect while you're in a setting for learning is emotionally taxing. It's easy to say 'beauty is on the inside' when most settings and conversations criticize another person's appearance. To fit in initially, you take on some of the personality traits of your friends.

Peer Pressure and Bullying

Your friends often tease you about how you're a little overweight. The off-hand remarks such as, 'You should go to the gym more,' and, 'You should go on the same diet with us' overwhelm you. Or, they can insult you and your appearance by calling you vulgar and unnecessary names.

When the leader of the group decides to follow a fad or enforce a strict diet regimen, it's also creating hardships for you as well. No one wants to be ostracized, so they follow the leader's suggestions, even if it could be out of character for them. The same can be said about you as well. When your friends are peer pressuring you group dieting and falling into the habit of strict calorie intake, it's also affecting you.

Perhaps your friends are the reason for your bulimia. With the constant pressure to be skinny and look the best in your school, expectations are high. As we discussed heavily in the previous chapter, other people's insurmountable expectations of you can cause an eating disorder. Not only are the pressures coming from the unspoken rules of high school itself, but the peer pressure and blatant bullying from your friends is another source of high expectations.

Peer Pressure to Count Your Calories

Your purges may not look like the stereotypical 'throw up in the bathroom after a meal', but instead could be reflected in the new obsession with calorie-counting. Your friends have started a new diet that they found on TikTok promoting weight loss. One of your friends has parents who are health-conscious and are always talking to their children about the importance of dieting for a healthy lifestyle.

Your friends may have convinced you that you, too, need to lose weight. They point out all the flaws in your appearance while simultaneously harassing you about the food you eat. They pressure you into not eating as much while still counting your calories to prevent overeating. To slim down, you start eating less and less. The fewer calories you eat, the more weight you lose.

Potentially Fatal Flaws

Significant time has passed, and now your weight is the least it's ever been. Everyone compliments you on how skinny you are, and how great you look, but inside you feel like the trash on the side of the curb. You're hungry for food, real food, and to keep it inside your stomach like you used to.

For me, being on the cheerleading team and having a boyfriend who played football caused me to have high visibility in the realm of high school. Everyone thought I had an amazing figure and would even compliment me on it. On the inside, I felt awful. I wanted to eat the foods I could before instead of a meager Slim Fast shake in the morning, a Slim Fast bar at lunch, and eating a caesar salad with my family at dinner for years before getting help. Nausea and heartburn swept over me as I ate; afterward, I would make myself sick.

Compliments Were My Prison

Compliments might seem like a good thing, but they were detrimental to me while I was in school. In the context of my eating disorder, compliments actually perpetuated the cycle of consumption and purging. According to a study conducted by Amy Slater and Marika Tiggerman, '...results suggest that positive appearance-related comments (compliments) may be just as, or even more, likely to give rise to self-objectification as negative appearance-related comments' (2014). While I was afraid of not looking skinny enough, the compliments acted as validation for my disorder to continue.

Because of the compliments on my figure, I knew I had to maintain this cycle of eating and purging. What they didn't see, however, was how I abused my body to maintain my figure. Even though I felt horrible, I couldn't contain the amount of pressure I placed on myself through the external validations of other people as I started to lose weight in an unhealthy way. The compliments I received turned to daggers as I tried to maintain their expectations.

The comments kept me in the same mental space for years as my condition and deterioration increased. I was imprisoned by their comments because people don't realize that their comments have an impact on others. The external validation I received prompted my disorder to become even worse.

Because of my frequent trips to the bathroom, it was hard for me to even think about going out to parties or friends' houses to hang out. Similar to you, my eating disorder was my source of shame, and I needed to keep it from everyone around me.

THE DREAD OF SOCIALIZATION

As you start to withdraw from your friend group and further isolate yourself, the thought of interacting with your friends outside of school is like lead in your stomach. You don't want to be around other people right now in the state you're in. Panicking, you tell them you're not sure and you'll have to ask your parents. It's not quite a lie, but it's one that your friends will believe to give you time to think over the pros and cons.

The momentary dread you feel in your stomach has lifted, but you've already said no a few times beforehand. This social obligation you feel is daunting. You're exhausted enough as it is; after all, you're just not feeling that well. Your eating disorder is beating you down. Your friends will need an answer the next day, so time is of the essence.

To Socialize, Or Not to Socialize?

Sleepovers, game nights, and even just hanging out fill you with immense dread. No matter the situation of socialization, you're putting yourself at risk of someone potentially finding out your secret. The burden of bulimia weighs on you as you decipher the pros and cons. You have so many questions that need answering, but you can't ask the specifics of them. Sure, you can ask some things, such as the types of food, but it's the other questions, the hard-hitters, that could potentially give away your eating disorder. Questions such as:

- What food, if any, will be there?
- Will I be able to keep it down long enough for the party to be over?
- How can I hide my frequent bathroom visits without rousing suspicion from my friends?
- Is there more than one bathroom, and are they easily accessible?
- Do they know, and they're just waiting to catch me in the act?
- Who else is going to be there?
- Do I even want to hang out with these so-called friends anymore when all I want to do is be alone?

Instead of having a 'normal' high school experience, I was instead sheltering myself inside the sanctuary of the bathroom and my room, or I was volunteering at the hospital. My friends, in turn, started to withdraw from me as well.

Your friends may not necessarily understand the implications behind the way you're acting all of a sudden, but it's concerning them enough to make remarks to you. However, you've hurt their feelings, so they lash out at you instead of acknowledging the problem. Your emotions are haywire, and you can't seem to focus on a lot of things anymore. Your emotions shift daily, and it's come to the point where they ask you one question:

'Are You Bipolar Or Something?'

The constant fluctuations of moods are not something your friends are normally accustomed to. Every teenager's emotions tend to fluctuate, as can be expected, but your range of emotions has completely gone haywire. You're happy one morning when you come into school, sad the next day, and then rage the day after that. There is no pattern to your behavior and your emotions. The question on everyone's mind and their lips was, 'Are you bipolar or something?'

Once you reflect on the question and how you answered with denial, you realize that you were deflecting because you didn't know how to answer the question. As you learned in Chapter 1, bulimia is a consequence of the inability to regulate your emotions. Since you are preoccupied with only maintaining your figure and nothing else, the cracks start to form and show. You begin to lash out at those around you in a vain attempt to preserve your secret.

No One Believes Me

As the cracks in your foundation start to form into chasms, you have also created a rift between yourself and your friends, to the point where they no longer believe the things you tell them.

When you do decide to open up to your friends, they may recoil from you. Some might even claim that you're making a sick joke or that this is your grasp for even more attention. In some cases, their blatant jealousy towards you for receiving the attention they desire blocks any understanding of the reason behind your slim figure. Some may resent you for pulling away from them; therefore they no longer support you and your deceit.

The friends you once had vanished as quickly as they came. You no longer have a best friend because she is so hurt that you've kept this secret from her. Some of your other friends have backed off because of the stigma still against people living with bulimia. Others may have heard through the grapevine of your disorder, but they refuse to acknowledge it or try to help you in any way. The girls who were initially jealous of the attention you had, thought it was a cry for more attention. The names these girls call you can ruin your reputation for the rest of your high school career. There are very few who try to help.

While this last example may appear to be extreme, it can be the case for you. Every situation and every teenage girl is unique with vastly different life experiences. I never experienced ostracization from my high school except for the self-imposed isolation. Nevertheless, I was ashamed of myself and felt guilty for keeping my friends in the dark about my disorder for so long.

GUILT PROLONGING

Guilt and feeling ashamed are major staples of bulimia. From the inability to keep food down and wasting food, to the necessity for secret-keeping, bulimia has caused you to become a shell of the girl you used to be. You are not only feeling guilty for the uncontrollable urge to maintain a specific figure, but you're also grieving the girl you used to be.

Grief and guilt often walk beside each other in many facets of life. When someone we love passes away, part of the grieving process is feeling guilty and ashamed of not spending a lot of time with that person before their passing.

In a way, you are grieving the young, carefree girl you used to be. Along the way to your downward spiral of bulimia, you've lost yourself in the endless cycle of bulimia and weight control. The grief you feel wraps around the guilt of not treating your friends, family, and yourself with the respect and love they deserve. This is unfortunately a way for our brains to process the emotions of loss, confusion, and helplessness.

The cycle of feeling these intense emotions can have you wallowing in the depths of despair. I know exactly how you feel to have this immense loss of identity to a disorder that you can no longer control. For me, what started in middle school between the ages of 11-13 lasted until my last years of high school. The waves of sorrow and pain from my past with bulimia are ripples I still feel to this day. Recovery will be one of the hardest things you'll have to do to date, but it's a result worth the journey and roadblocks along the way. Your future self will be thanking you for not giving up on her.

Now that we've talked about the effects of interpersonal relationships with bulimia, let's shift our focus to how the media can be the negative turning point for those who will start their downward spiral with bulimia.

SOCIETAL AND MEDIA PRESSURES

Societal and media pressures are by far one of the worst influences that promote the behaviors of bulimia. In between the societal pressures and now the influx of social media engagement on our phones, there isn't a day that flies by without the bombardment of fatphobic themes and messages. Most of these types of messages are aimed directly at young girls who, according to society and social media standards, should be skinny to be considered beautiful and healthy.

I've mentioned previously that the idea of being skinny does not equate to being healthy. I often wish I could go back in time to tell my younger self that she was more than her appearance. She was smart and brave. And so are you. You're not defined by the number on a scale.

The Time Before Social Media

Before the introduction of media as we think of today such as television and print, the weight of a woman was indicative of her socioeconomic status. Women who were heavier were considered to be the best option for marriage. If a woman was overweight, it was indicative of a surplus of food. Her family was of higher socioeconomic status; thin women were considered poor and of the peasant class. Society dictates what is popular and acceptable, which then bleeds through into normal life and the principles that are set.

With the introduction of print, and then eventually television, the societal rules were often rooted in marketing campaigns such as advertisements and even through media such as newspapers, television programs, and film. The need for women to be skinny was the pinnacle of health; these concepts were not fully readily available to those who were illiterate in the case of newspapers and other forms of print to the public until the introduction of television and film when actresses played key roles. Hollywood is a major benefactor in the insurgence of eating disorders such as bulimia and anorexia. Once these women became famous, they were also role models for women and generations to come. To become supermodels or actresses, they had to be attractive. At the time, to be young and skinny with a beautiful face done in makeup were the norms.

The pressures to be young, skinny, and beautiful were the faces of marketing campaigns for beauty products as well as fashion. Actresses who were young and skinny often were seen in the commercials in between the television programs. How women perceived their bodies correlates to the cultural changes throughout the years. According to Ana Paula Gonçalves de Oliveira, 'Publicity influences the promotion and appreciation of having a body within the standards of beauty spread today, thus, there is an increase in the search for the idealized' (2020). Because of this widespread need to possess the ideal body, for some adolescent girls, it was necessary to take the extreme route of eating disorders.

This is especially true in adolescents who use social media, and the women portrayed in the media as role models for body standards. To conform to the set standards, they dive into bulimia despite its health risks. 'In order to feel themselves belonging to the social environment and to perceive a positive self-image, they choose to change their eating behavior drastically' (Copetti and Quiroga 2018). Adolescents well into adulthood feel this implicit pull to skinniness because of the media they consume.

The Influence of Social Media

Social media is also a huge culprit for bulimia and other eating disorders drastically increasing. Teenagers and young adults tend to use their cell phones more than the previous generations. Because of the introduction to smartphones and the accessibility to having constant access to content no matter where you are, it's easy to lose yourself in the clutches of the internet.

Many studies have been conducted on social media and the emergence of bulimia and other eating disorders. These studies have concluded that teenagers like yourself and the influx of eating disorders such as bulimia positively correlate. With so much content online, it's now easier to send and receive messages regarding body shaming and fatphobia. The necessity to point out flaws in a person such as weight can cause drastic life changes such as relying on bulimia to have the perfect figure.

Now, I'm not saying to completely delete apps such as Instagram and TikTok from your phone; in the end, that is completely your decision. Social media can be useful in rallying against someone who is body shaming you online. You can even belong to groups and follow those who are open about their struggles with bulimia and other disorders. With so much information online, you learn something new every day and have the accessibility to have support in a time when you feel isolated from the people around you.

If deleting the apps off your phone can lead you to steps toward peace, then it's always a suggestion. In the end, we all deserve some tranquility. Because you're struggling with so much at such a young age, you deserve to have some peace too.

ALL I WANT IS PEACE

I know how exhausted you are from struggling and fighting to have some peace within your life. Having bulimia is a hard disorder to endure, and even more troublesome to overcome. It's exhausting to tell lies or remain quiet when someone asks you why you're in the bathroom for so long or why you go to the gym for such a long time. One of the main things is that you lost yourself along the way trying to accomplish an unrealistic lifestyle.

You're scared and you feel as though you're alone in this world right now. You picked up this book for a reason. I want to remind you that you're not alone. There are so many of us who are just like you and experienced some of the things you have. We will talk more about how to gain your way to peace, but for now, I'm glad you've started to take the steps towards recovery.

You deserve to eat the food you want to without feeling guilty about it. But most importantly, you deserve to have peace.

KEY TAKEAWAYS

This chapter mainly focused on the outward appearance of your friends and to the rest of the world through social media. The balance between school, your friends and family, and your role in society is tricky to maneuver even at your best. To condense everything you've learned in this chapter, here are some key takeaways.

- Your friends often ignore the problem that has become so transparent now that you've lost some weight.
- The frequent visits to the bathroom are one of the reasons they are starting to catch on to your eating disorder. They may have suspicions, but they may also be waiting for you to come to them about the problem.
- In between the constant hydration and the newfound love for healthy food such as salads, you are making it easy for them to discover your secret.
- Because of your disorder, you have managed to convince yourself that no one cares for you, so you start to withdraw from your friends.
- The influence of your friends highly impacts your eating disorder and how you cope with it. It's

important to reflect on your friendships to find out what kind of people they are.

- You may realize that your friends constantly bully and peer pressure you into behaviors that can lead to bulimia such as obsessive calorie-counting.
- This peer pressure from your friends is a major factor in the development of your disorder.
- The potentially fatal flaws within your friends have rubbed off on you.
- The compliments you receive on your figure now that you've lost weight only perpetuates the need to overindulge in food and then purge it later. Compliments once made you feel amazing, but now they only instill the need to look skinny to feel loved.
- Parties, sleepovers, game nights, and other forms of social interaction with others are now something you dread. When invited, you obsess over many different things such as if it would be noticeable if you stole away for a while instead of looking forward to the time you would be spending with your friends.
- You often must weigh the pros and cons of whether to go or not. Nowadays, your friends don't invite you to go places anymore because you no longer attend any functions.
- You are often questioned if you're bipolar because of the varying moods you have daily.
- When you do open up to your friends, very few of them believe you because they're jealous you receive more attention than they do.
- All of this prolongs your guilt. Grief and guilt often walk hand-in-hand with each other while simultaneously feeding off of you.

- The pressures of society and the use of social media have increased the number of sufferers of eating disorders such as bulimia.
- The only thing you truly want is peace.

With the surplus of information in this chapter, it's important to take note of how your friends treat you. Remember that once you open up to them about your disorder, a true friend will believe you and find ways to help you. Maintaining the balance of friends, family, and how society values you based on your weight can be a lot to handle. But what about extracurricular activities? Read on to the next chapter to learn about how the environment you're in will promote your eating disorder.

5

EXTRACURRICULARS

I mentioned before how I was a cheerleader and my boyfriend at the time was on the high school football team. As you can imagine, being a cheerleader led to so many expectations that were self-imposed such as weight consciousness. The unbearable societal pressures on me as a cheerleader bled into every facet of my life including academics. Not only was I on the cheerleading squad, but the fact I excelled academically put a ridiculous weight of expectations on me. For you, the after-school extracurriculars your school offers may be different, but with no fewer expectations. Perhaps you're in a private school that offers more sports or high-tech classes than a public school.

Maybe you're in the school play they put on every year, or there's a robotics class you're interested in but have yet to sign up for. In various schools depending on funding from the state and private donations, what you have available to you can either be extremely limited or full of opportunity. If there are more options, you have more outlets to experiment in. If there's an issue with funding such as budget cuts in the arts, the school may not have those options available to you.

Fortunately, there are always opportunities to create an environment that promotes learning and, in your case, healing from bulimia. We will cover more about carefully selecting the type of environment to promote recovery in the next chapter; for now, it's necessary to learn how your environment affects you.

The extracurriculars you're involved with, if you are at all, can either help or hinder your progress towards recovery. The environment from an emotional, as well as a physical standpoint, impacts mental health by encouraging certain behaviors and providing a structure for learning. However, there can be some instances where extracurricular activities promote the cycle of bulimia.

THE IMPORTANCE OF ENVIRONMENT

Take a moment to reflect on the environment of your extracurriculars as both a physical and emotional space. Is the physical space disorganized or clean and organized to find the materials and necessary equipment you need? The physical space of the environment impacts you on an emotional level as well. If the physical space is disorganized, your thoughts will be as well. Disorganized spaces can also lead to feeling overwhelmed, and therefore you are at risk of purging. However, if the space is clean and organized, you may feel more at ease in your surroundings and your emotional state.

The same is true for the emotional space. Are your peers helpful toward the end goal such as beating the other team in sports or, in the case of the previous example, are the other art students constructive in their criticism? Are your coaches or teachers and peers respectful toward you? These are questions to consider when choosing an extracurricular to ensure your steps toward recovery instead of relapse.

Different environments and people create a new headspace as you navigate through various clubs and activities within your school or even private lessons. For example, an art studio is an entirely different environment than a sports team. A writing workshop is a polar opposite of being on a debate team or a robotics team. Each activity creates a unique environment and headspace that reflects it.

Some Activities Promote Bulimia and Emotional Withdrawal

When you change your surroundings, your perspective shifts as well. If there is only one thing you do outside of school, such as playing sports or holing yourself in your room playing video games, your perspectives stagnate. Introducing yourself to another form of activity can help you on your journey in recovery. We'll discover more activities and how to choose those specific ones in the next chapter.

Some of these activities promote bulimia and social withdrawal. For example, if you're on a sports team that requires relentless physical activity and working out to maintain a certain level of fitness, this sport may not be the correct place for you during your recovery. This can be especially true if your bulimia revolves around either obsessively counting calories or extreme levels of workout.

Sports are not the only culprit with the onset of bulimia. Other highly competitive extracurriculars such as the debate team or even the chess club can be benefactors to your eating disorder. The presence of ruthless competition and your anxiety over competing can allude to developing bulimia.

Negative Circumstances

Be mindful of the friends you have around you. While friendships were covered in the last chapter, it's also crucial to watch out for those who could be considered negative influences, especially in the realm of dangerous situations. The dangerous situations don't necessarily have to be life-threatening. It can also create implications of dangers to your mental health, and therefore could increase the symptoms of bulimia by engaging in risky behaviors.

Although the negative environments can deeply encourage the onset and continuation of bulimia, it can also be noted that happy occasions can also affect your perception of body image as well.

HAPPY OCCASIONS, SKEWED BODY IMAGE

Happy occasions, however, don't necessarily guarantee that the symptoms of bulimia you are experiencing leaves. On the contrary, they can lead to an overanalysis of your body. An exciting opportunity such as making the lacrosse team, gaining a leadership position in the club you've been a part of for a while, or even your crush asking you to the prom can negatively impact your analysis of your body and how your clothes fit.

I was able to volunteer at a hospital while in high school, and I excelled academically. But I was isolated from the kids I went to school with and within my family. To take my mind off the doom of loneliness, I volunteered at the local hospital. While this was an exciting opportunity for me, the isolation I felt further invited the cycle of bulimia. It was as if no one cared about me. I spent most of my time alone when not volunteering at the hospital by doing pilates and plunging into my academics. Spending a lot of time on self-reflection and improving myself eventually led me onto the journey to recovery. However, the isolation I felt reinforced my low self-image because it felt as though no one wanted me around them.

The Voices of Your Self-Image

The isolation I experienced at such a young age reinforced every flaw I had, especially revolving around my weight. The inner voices hounded me to comb through every part of my body and hyperfixate on them. My thighs were too thick; my belly pudge extended over my waistline. I was too big, and I needed to lose the weight I had gained. Throughout my journey with bulimia, the compliments I received both cemented the action of losing weight and confirmed that my inner voices were correct. Even though I practiced self-reflection every day, it was difficult to improve my self-worth.

Bulimia calls upon the darkest parts of your mind as you over analyze every facet of your life. It creates negative self-talk as you internalize all the antagonistic voices that you've heard in between the comments and expectations others have placed on you. As a result, the inner voice wins you over as you critique every part of your body. It tramples any hope that you can muster, shoving it out of your mind. Like a plague, the inner voices sweep through your mind and infect it with every possible negative outcome and the hyper analysis of your self-worth and body.

For example, your crush asked you to go to the homecoming dance. It's the moment you've been waiting for since you both have been texting back and forth and flirting in between classes. You should be ecstatic, and you are. In addition to the initial excitement, the cold dread stops you from feeling all the positive emotions. Your mother, who is supportive and wants you to have the best time at the dance, takes you shopping for the perfect outfit. She whisks you off to your favorite department store with all the cute clothes and outfits that would be perfect for this special occasion.

The only thing you can think about is how you'll look in the outfit. Your mind whirls from 'Will I look okay?' to 'Will your crush like how you look in this dress?' Instead of knowing you'll look amazing in the outfit, you're preoccupied with how to get away from the inevitable purges that will happen throughout the night. Your eating disorder perpetuates your perception of a skewed body image.

Scathing Self-Doubt

While the dance was only an example, many other opportunities present themselves in need of celebration. Self-doubt manifests in anyone at any given time, but those who suffer from eating disorders such as bulimia are much more prone to them compared to the typical teenager. Constant reassurance with compliments of your figure from others as well as obsessively checking yourself in the mirror is the harbinger of self-doubt and low self-esteem.

Another example is when you make the winning basket for your basketball team, and now you're all going to the state finals. Everyone is thrilled because you were the reason for your team to move forward into the finals. As a result, your coach, team, teachers, and even parents rejoice by calling out your name. You may even think that you don't deserve the praise; after all, it was a team effort. Instead of taking all the credit, you shove it aside and only focus on how you could have improved your game. Your low self-esteem is causing you to fake humility, and therefore you are unable to accept the praise.

Just because happy occasions are the positive boost you need to combat the disorder you're struggling with, it doesn't necessarily mean that your life is about to drastically change. One happy moment in the long list of negative experiences will not be your defining moment in beating the disorder, but it can be a step towards your journey to recovery.

DISAPPOINTING MOMENTS

When the doors to opportunities close, it can be extremely difficult to navigate through the feeling of not feeling good enough. You already experience so much pressure with academics, family, and social interactions. When opportunities are missed, the impulse to internalize why you weren't good enough for the role or position overwhelms you, poisoning your mind into thinking you are not valuable.

I had an older sister attend the same high school as me. You'd think that as sisters, we'd bond over the same teachers and experiences at the high school. We should have stuck together through thick and thin, but that simply wasn't the case. She never really wanted me around and took any opportunity to talk over me while I was speaking to her and her friends. To impress her friends and the other people around her, she often told me, 'No one wants to hear you speak, Shannon.'

These types of remarks from my sister deeply wounded me and furthered my descent into my eating disorder. It could be the same for you in your family system, or even from your peers and society in general repeatedly informing you that you're not welcome. While I was upset with her for the verbal abuse, that same abuse further caused my isolation and low self-worth. If my sister didn't want me around, why would other people?

These sad moments in my life where it felt as though my sister didn't want me around her made me believe that I was a failure. I internalized what she said to me at school and continued to self-isolate from her. As much as I wanted her to be a part of my life, she acted and voiced her cruelty towards me and prevented us from having a decent relationship during school hours.

Her public rejection of me during school wounded me. While I often self-reflected during pilates and my alone time, this failure of maintaining a relationship with my sister during my teenage years affected me. The rejections of my sister and the hurt it caused may be similar to your experiences of the rejections of your peers and missed opportunities.

Failures and Setbacks

Maybe your debate team didn't elect you as their leader, or you didn't get the leadership position you applied for in the club you've played a major role in for three years. Perhaps you didn't get one of the solos in glee club. No matter what the circumstance is for your situation, the rejection from it is a deep wound. Rejection hurts for everyone, but for those of us who struggle with low self-esteem and self-worth, it's a wake-up call to the delusion that we're going to excel in everything we do.

While rejection and disappointment can feel like a deep personal wound, when we turn that disappointment and rejection inward, it creates the ongoing cycle of bulimia. I won't say to not feel those feelings; it's human and natural for those feelings to present themselves to us. But don't allow yourself to wallow in those depths for longer than necessary. Remember, you are not defined by your failures. How you learn and grow from those failures and setbacks will determine who you are.

Think for a moment about a time you were rejected or failed at something. How did you deal with those failures and setbacks as someone who struggles with bulimia? What events triggered you to purge? Frame them into learning experiences instead of internalizing them. It's easier said than done, but with the right support system and engagement in other extracurriculars, it will help you further down the line.

When you turn those failures inwards and do not live up to the expectations placed on you, you're reintroducing the cycle of impulse eating and purging. You're reinforcing the contract between wants versus needs, and the cycle continues.

THE SOCIAL CONTRACT

When you feel disappointed, rejected, or hurt, it leads to an emotional craving for large quantities of your favorite foods. Afterward, you feel ashamed and embarrassed of your consumption of extra calories, which then ushers in the need to purge.

The contract of wants versus needs is a social one when the contract concerns bulimia. Because social performance can weigh just as heavily on your mind as much as academics, the result is exactly the same. There are unrealistic expectations and normalness forced on you in the context of how you should present yourself to those around you. You're young and impressionable at this point in your life; it's not your fault that these expectations are forced on you. I felt the same as you when I was in high school. Whether the expectations are placed on you by fellow students or advertisements on social media sites, they are still present in daily life.

These same societal pressures to fit in and to present yourself as normal to the rest of the world affect us all. When we feel like we're an outcast, especially those of us who suffer from eating disorders such as bulimia, the need to belong is at a heightened state. You want to close yourself to the societal pressures of the lie of 'skinny equals beautiful and valued', so you need to purge to make that happen for you.

I Just Want To Fit In

It's human nature to want to fit in and be accepted for who you are. During our high school years, we start to figure out who we are and the people we want to associate with. We all transition from different phases as we learn and understand ourselves. Some high schoolers transition from being preppy to their goth phase, while others experiment with other phases such as being the quiet kid in the back of the class to becoming part of the popular kids in school. Personalities will shift throughout this time in your life. High school is full of change, and there are a rare few who are truly comfortable with themselves.

According to the psychological theory called Maslow's hierarchy of needs, the need to belong in society is in the third tier above physical needs, such as food, water, and shelter, and the need of feeling safe. We all want to fit in and need to feel loved, accepted, and respected for who we are. It's instilled in us to have a sense of community and to feel like we belong.

For those who suffer from bulimia, it can be difficult to fulfill this third tier in the hierarchy of needs because of low self-esteem and self-worth. When you're feeling down about your body and overwhelmed by all the expectations thrown at you, feeling that same love, respect, and acceptance is an uphill battle. You know what you need, but to achieve this need, you overextend yourself to fulfill the expectations that are placed on you by society, your peers, and your family.

The Harsh Lens of Self-Perception

You're constantly at war with yourself in the context of what you want versus what you need. It's challenging for most people to distinguish these two concepts in daily life, but for the sufferers of bulimia such as yourself, the fine line between these concepts is often blurred or completely skewed. For example, you have an inherent need to feel acceptance and belonging from your peers, which is completely understandable. However, when your peers follow the societal pressures to be skinny, that 'want' to become skinny morphs into a 'need'. Once this new 'need' is established, it then leads an entryway to the cycle of bulimia.

This skewed perception of wants versus needs then translates to impulse eating and purging. When the 'want' becomes a 'need', the cycle begins. This new need to fit in with your peers then transforms your thinking into how you perceive yourself. You begin to only see your shell and what others think of it, not the value of the person you are. You absorb the same beliefs and expectations of those around you and start to gaze at yourself through the same harsh lens.

This new harsh lens is now how you view yourself. The pressures from outside of yourself have now pivoted and aimed themselves toward your self-perception. You can no longer fight off the new 'need' to be skinny; as a result, you obsess over your weight and how your clothes fit on you. Your newly discovered flaws must now be covered and managed through extreme instances of purging. Your 'want' and your 'need' are officially distorted and have dire physical and mental health consequences. Some examples of this are:

- I want to fit in, so I need to get this food out of me.
- I wanted my favorite food and ate too much, so now I feel too heavy and need to purge.
- I wanted this food that had too many calories, so now I need to get rid of it.

These examples may even be a part of your relationship with food currently. Reflect on your wants and needs in the context of your disorder. What are your current 'wants' and 'needs'? How did you view yourself before the introduction of bulimia, and how did that change once the cycle began? Understanding yourself and figuring out the shift in wants and needs as you developed bulimia will help guide you later on as you implement the steps to healing.

KEY TAKEAWAYS

The environment that surrounds you can either be a place full of positivity and healing or a detriment to your recovery and may cause relapse. You've picked up this book for a reason; to understand more about your eating disorder and how to navigate your way through it. This chapter granted you access to a deep dive into extracurriculars, the environment within them, and the implications of negative self-talk. With so much compacted into one chapter, it's necessary to highlight the key takeaways for reflection and implementation.

- The environment that surrounds you can either be a positive or a negative influence on you. The term 'environment' not only relates to a physical space but an emotional one as well. What is encouraged in your environment is what will continue.
- Extracurricular activities can help with healing and recovery, especially in the context of mental health and bulimia.
- Some of these extracurricular activities, however, can promote bulimia and emotional withdrawal such as sports if the sufferer of bulimia excessively exercises as a purge.
- Negative circumstances and environments perpetuate the cycle of eating and then purging. It's necessary to reflect on the types of environments your extracurriculars are in, especially if they are dangerous and potentially life-threatening.
- While happy occasions appear to be a time of celebration, they can also amplify the over analyzation of your body and weight.
- The inner voices in your head convince you that no matter what you're doing and accomplishing, your weight and body image is the only thing that matters. You've become too preoccupied with your body perception that the initial excitement of the achievement is just another stressor for you.
- Because of the immense pressure that you have placed on yourself, you're incapable of feeling confident in your abilities. Instead, the scathing remarks of your self-doubt plague you, and you're unable to fully embrace the celebration.
- There will be disappointing and heartbreaking moments during your high school career. However,

when you suffer from bulimia, you internalize these disappointments and frame them as failures.

- You will experience failure and setbacks in your teenage years. As is the same for disappointment, you turn that failure inwards and see yourself as a permanent failure. Rejection is painful, but don't allow yourself to internalize those feelings to use as fuel for continuing the cycle of eating and purging.
- There is an inherent need for everyone to feel as though they belong to a group. Your wants and needs are muddled and twisted, and you confuse your deep needs with temporary wants.
- Everyone wants to fit in, and one of your ways of doing so is through the onset of bulimia. This contract between wants and needs is how you navigate through the social pressures placed on you during your high school years.
- You often see yourself through the harsh lens of self-perception. You're constantly thinking about your weight and that number on a scale represents you as a person. It doesn't at all. You are worth so much more than your weight and perception of being skinny.

This is the last chapter concerning the information about bulimia. You've learned so much about how your environment, family, friends, and society have negatively impacted you and encouraged the onset of your disorder. It's crucial to know and reflect on your individual experiences while also learning how they can affect others as well. Knowing and understanding your motives will help you throughout your recovery process.

My stories of how I struggled have hopefully helped you realize that I do care and that you're not alone. I know the pain you feel firsthand, and I want to encourage and help you on the path to healing. The next chapter will be about the steps to healing and some recovery tips and tricks that I've learned.

6

STEPS TOWARD PEACE

*I*n the previous chapters, you've had to absorb a lot of information regarding the eating disorder bulimia. You are currently facing dark times, in the depths of despair from the monstrous cycle of bulimia. The unrealistic expectations of academics, social life, and home life are thrust upon you by your parents and society as a whole. You're on a path to self-destruction, and you know you need help. The cycle of purging has become an instinct when food or life itself becomes too heavy of a burden.

Just as with any dark time, there is always a light. You must keep going through the darkness to find it. On your journey with bulimia, there is also a long road to recovery that you can take. What's important here is to take it slow and make small ripples of change to make life-changing waves. You have a deep inner strength, and that strength combined with the will to change is what will see you through your journey to healing.

BABY STEPS

On the road to healing, you will encounter many bumps that may make you want to return to the habits of eating and then purging. There will be days that are more mentally exhausting because you're no longer relying on your crutch. However, you must keep pushing through to fully achieve the recovery you desperately need.

I know you have that inner strength within you to keep on the path to healing. When we're at the lowest point of our lives, that's when we are the most open to transformations. Since you've picked this book, you are in the process of realizing things need to change. You're cognizant enough to recognize a major modification is necessary to better your life and conditions. Your reasons are yours, but the fact that you're in this state of mind of things needing to change, means you're in the beginning stages of healing and recovery.

The key is to take tiny steps. Your recovery is a journey and will take both time and patience. You shouldn't change everything in one moment hoping for a drastic change in your life. There are behaviors to unlearn, relationships with food to be re-established, and the continuation of implementing what you've learned about yourself and steps that must be taken to achieve a full recovery. There will be mountains to climb, valleys to descend, and at the end will be the new you. Your future self will thank you for your recovery and the time you took to take care of yourself.

I won't lie: the road to recovery can be a long, bumpy ride. There will be setbacks you'll encounter from within yourself and those around you. You may have to let go of some of your previous friends because you've realized they're only perpetuating your disorder. It's the same as growing into adulthood when you conclude your inner peace of mind is more important than the pressures placed on you. When you let go of the people, ideologies, and environments holding you back, your life opens to new realms of opportunity.

REFRAME YOUR MINDSET

One of the first things you'll need to accomplish is learning how to reframe your thinking and perception of yourself. This first step is by far one of the hardest things you'll have to overcome as you recover. As much as you wish you could snap your fingers and the result will come, it, unfortunately, doesn't work like that. However, you can make waves out of ripples with small tweaks in your daily life.

Practice Positive Self-Talk

Practicing positive self-talk is as simple as looking in the mirror and telling yourself that you're beautiful the way you are. At first, you might feel silly but move forward through the feelings of discomfort and awkwardness. I won't give you a set number of how many times a day you should practice this but try it at least once a day in the privacy of your room if you have a mirror.

Take a deep breath and relax, look yourself in the eyes and say, 'You're beautiful and I love you'. This is especially important when you start to point out the flaws in your body. Take a step back from negative self-talk and replace it with something you like about yourself. Instead of 'Your stomach looks especially big today', tell yourself, 'I love the way your eyes shift colors' or 'I love how you aced that math test today.' Once you start practicing this in the mirror, it will eventually reframe your thinking about how you look and the perception of yourself. Positivity leads to more positivity, and soon you will be able to fight the urges to purge.

Journaling

Writing in general is an amazing stress reliever. It helps you gain the ability to express yourself in a way that's beneficial to you. The best part about journaling is that when you're writing, it's your safe space to unleash any feelings and emotions you normally are unable to process. You don't even have to be 'good' at it; you can just pick up your favorite writing utensil and vent your frustrations.

Journaling doesn't have to be solely venting frustrations; it can also be used as a way to organize your thinking and prioritize elements of life that are important to you. A great way to prioritize self-care and promote positive thinking is to write down what you're thankful for. A gratitude journal is simply a list of the things you're grateful for. I recommend writing at least five specific events that happened in the day. For example, an event could be, 'I am grateful for my friend refraining from speaking about my weight'. The event doesn't necessarily need to revolve around your struggle with bulimia; it could even be any other form of positive interaction. Listing the positives of the day will counter any negative thoughts that try to tackle you into submission.

The benefits of gratitude journaling can help you reframe your mind about yourself and your perception of the world as a whole. Psychologists have conducted many studies on the benefits of gratitude as a guide to a more positive outlook. I won't be able to fully explain the neuroscience behind gratitude in this book, but studies have shown that gratitude increases well-being and positivity. The benefits, according to authors Michael Eid and Randy J. Larson of the book *The Subjective Science of Well-Being*, are that '...gratitude strengthens social relationships...counters negative states... and...is a resiliency factor in times of stress' (479). Expressing gratitude both within a journal or even spoken aloud can drastically change the perception of yourself. By focusing inward on positivity, you'll experience higher self-esteem, a decrease in body dissatisfaction, and overall happiness. Both the long-term and short-term benefits will help you on your path to inner peace and eventual happiness.

Although gratitude journaling is a great way to alleviate stress and has important short-term and long-term benefits, it's not a substitute for getting professional help from a therapist or a counselor. Therapy is a useful tool in your toolkit that can help you change your perception of yourself as you recover.

GETTING HELP

We have now arrived at arguably the most crucial stage in overcoming your eating disorder: getting the help you need and deserve. Outside help from your support system or a therapist or counselor will guide you on your path to recovery and healing. At this point, you'll have to admit you have a problem not only with yourself but with the people who love you. It's a terrifying thought to open up about your struggles with bulimia, but I promise you that you will need them if you start to stray from your path. There is no shame in allowing the people who love you to help you. It's the opposite. Permitting yourself to be vulnerable and opening up about your experiences alludes to your inner strength. Getting help is also part of the healing and recovery process.

Don't allow your shame and guilt over having bulimia to leave you out in the cold. There are a lot of negative emotions whirling through you as you try to unpack your disorder. The impending conversations with your parents and friends followed by embarrassment and shame can be expected. *None of that matters when you open up to the people who love you.* Disregard your feelings of fear and embarrassment when you commit to discussing your struggles with bulimia. You have the right to recover, and they also have the right to know about your eating disorder. It may initially upset the people you love, but I promise the people you want to surround yourself with as you recover won't be upset with you. They will only want to see you happy, healthy, and safe. Their support is what matters for your recovery. After you've had the difficult conversation, you will feel lighter because you'll no longer feel as though you're alone in your struggle. You will now have people in your corner rooting for you.

Although journaling and positive self-talk are tools to guide you, they can't replace the accountability and support you gain from talking to someone you trust about your experiences. You are worthy of love and respect not only for yourself but from others as well.

The importance of mental health and the lessening stigma of seeing a therapist or counselor is a move in the positive direction. Young people are recognizing the need to be able to talk to a neutral party about the struggles they're dealing with. This lessening stigma against counselors and therapists is making these resources much easier to access and utilize.

Therapy

Having a neutral party whose passion is to help people wade through the complexity of their emotions was extremely valuable to me. It allowed me to think and impose challenging self-reflection as a means to correct my unhealthy behaviors. It's crucial to self-reflect, but having another guide may help you beyond measure.

Seeing a therapist or counselor is a great way to move into another headspace altogether. A therapist will challenge your thinking and your perception of yourself. When choosing a therapist either locally or online, you are welcome to interview therapists and see who meshes the most with you and your personality as well as having expertise in eating disorders. You want someone who you're going to be comfortable opening up with and allowing your vulnerability to show.

The role of a therapist is not only to allow you to share your vulnerability and challenge you, but they are also a part of your support system. They kindly remind you of your worth. There will be times you'll want to skip a session. I felt that way a lot of times myself, especially when I first began the recovery process and spoke to my therapist. It will be better once you build a relationship based on trust.

One-on-one therapy may not work for everyone, however. Several issues can arise from the therapy sessions, such as not feeling comfortable seeking a therapist. There can be financial hurdles in place that may prevent your family from gaining access to a therapeutic one-on-one resource. If therapy sessions like this don't appeal to you or your family is struggling financially, there is another form of therapy that may prove useful to you.

Group Sessions

Group therapy is a more cost-effective form of therapy that can also prove beneficial to you. According to Lindsay T. Murn, group therapies encompass the same benefits as regular therapy in a more cost-efficient manner for the families of the sufferers (2010). Similar to other group therapies for other problems and disorders, the format of others listening to your experiences will help with your accountability as well as overcoming your feelings of isolation.

When you attend a group therapy session, I would recommend first listening to others. It can help clear up the question, 'Do I have a problem?' As you listen to their stories, you may be surprised to find similar symptoms, feelings, and reactions in others. The same experiences and feelings are fundamental to help you in your recovery process, deepening the affirmation that you're not alone.

In total, there are five theories of group therapy: self-help, psychodynamic, relational, psychoeducational, and cognitive behavioral therapy (CBT). Each type of group therapy has its strengths and weaknesses due to the individual sufferer's needs. For example, the relational theory of group therapy focuses on creating a balance between the sufferer of bulimia and the relationships around her, while self-help therapy gives the sufferer the option to have one-on-one conversations with someone who is further along in their journey. Studies have been conducted on each theory, demonstrating that no theory is more significant than the other. Because bulimia is so complex, no one way works best for everyone.

Group therapy sessions promote an open and honest form of communication as it combats the secrecy of your eating disorder. They also provide validation for your struggle with your eating disorder as well as give you the space to relearn how to form and build interpersonal relationships. Studies have shown that group therapies have helped many in their journey to overcoming bulimia because of its many benefits.

In addition to both individual and group therapies, leaving your comfort zone in a new environment can also help to remove old triggers and encourage recovery. The necessity of implementing positive extracurricular activities can help you regain confidence and a better relationship with yourself and food.

THE IMPORTANCE OF POSITIVE EXTRACURRICULARS

When you engage in positive forms of extracurricular activities, it will help you on your journey to healing and growth. Discovering a new outlet for your emotions as well as supplementing your want for the competition is one of the best ways to combat your feelings of shame, fear, and guilt. Exercising, discovering a new hobby and environment, or even finding love in music or art will help you on your journey.

I suggest utilizing at least one of the four activities explained below. These activities have helped me and so many others in your position. However, just as everyone is unique, so are the steps you take to achieve recovery. What works for others won't necessarily work for you, especially if there are triggers within some of the activities. Use that to your advantage as you use this time to rediscover yourself and the things you love to do. Don't be afraid to try new ideas and new ways of thinking. It could, quite literally, save your life.

Seek Out Different Environments

Bulimia sufferers often feel caught up in their daily activities and the stagnation of their lives. By seeking out new and different environments, you're not only avoiding and calming your triggers, but you're actively trying to change your life. You're in the process of recovery, but you're also in the process of rediscovering and reinventing yourself. This reinvention and recovery will require you to leave your comfort zone and explore the world around you.

I'm not saying to live in a completely different state or country, but simply open your mind to the rest of your city or town. What are the things you like to do or even enjoy? What are some things you haven't tried to do? Shake out the flat, stagnant daily life and explore other extracurricular activities around your city or town. Maybe you've always wanted to learn how to dance but always believed you had two left feet. Sign up for a dance class. Are there some books you've wanted to read but you're afraid of your friends poking fun at you for reading? Sign up for a book club at the local library. Maybe you've never played field hockey but your friends from your group therapy are playing. Go out and have fun!

Many activities can help you experience a different environment instead of remaining stuck in only one place. If you only gather information from one place, for example, your inner thoughts from bulimia become stale and rigid. However, experiencing and drawing conclusions from people who are different from you will help you heal and become whole.

Engaging in conversations with others from different backgrounds and being a part of something other than yourself will help you with your recovery. For so long, the expectations of perfection and being good at everything wears you down. Once you experience something new, the excitement for life returns. You're gazing less inward and more outward as you learn that perfection is overrated and that happiness, respect, and kindness are what you need and deserve.

Exercise

The first positive extracurricular activity is exercising. If exercising to the extreme is the way you purge, and reframe your thinking. Exercise encompasses so much more than playing a sport and going to the gym. It could be as simple as taking a late evening walk around the block either by yourself or even a hike in the mountains if there are any nearby.

Being in nature will help calm you and the inner turmoil within yourself.

Seeking out a non-school-related exercise will help you avoid the triggers and the need to prove yourself. Finding a group exercise can help you regulate your need to compete. For example, maybe the group therapy you're in may have basketball games twice a week at your local recreation center. Basketball isn't your sport, but you decide to give it a shot anyway. There is competition, yes, but there is also a support system that will be able to help you regain your confidence in your abilities.

If you feel yourself getting tired, either sit out for a while or simply walk away from the activity. The goal is to set up a new environment for you to feel supported and comfortable while maintaining control of your body and mind.

Self-care exercises such as walking on a treadmill, swimming, or even doing yoga will help you focus on yourself and control your body. If, after a yoga session you're feeling clearer and more at peace, do that same activity later again in the week. Introducing new, positive outlets for exercise will make a big difference in your recovery.

Meditation

Meditation can be beneficial to those who suffer from bulimia because it gives you a look inward without the chaos of the outside world. Focusing on your breathing in guided meditation or even doing yoga will help you learn breath control. When you learn breath control, it will make your emotions easier to control as well.

Self-reflection and self-awareness can be huge hurdles to cross as you first start to overcome your disorder. With meditation, either guided through YouTube channels or alone, you can look inward and figure out some of the reasons behind your disorder. Meditation will help you unlock the hidden secrets of yourself and open your mind to self-discovery.

Music and Art Therapy

Art therapy as a whole is a wonderful form of therapy. You might be picturing an art and crafts moment with teachers back in your elementary school days, but this art therapy is quite different. By 'art', I don't just mean drawing and painting, but music as well. Art gives us the ability to express ourselves that no other activity can. Writing, while also considered an art form, doesn't transcend language the same way as painting, drawing, or listening to music can, and this is the type of therapy I'll cover in this section.

Art therapy involves the act of creating art, such as drawing or painting. You don't have to be the next Picasso or van Gogh to create your masterpieces and self-expression. Even if you can't draw stick figures, start by drawing a simple line on the page and allow your imagination to take over. Break out the old art set your relatives would give you for Christmas and birthdays when you were in elementary school. Sharpen your colored pencils or crayons and create. Utilize the blank canvas, be it notebook paper or actual canvas, empty your mind of everything else but the task at hand, and let your imagination free itself. Even if it's simple squares and triangles, try to color them in. Draw funky shapes. Or, find your old coloring books and color the pages that stick out to you. But mainly, allow the emotions within you to be released onto the page. I promise you'll feel better afterward.

Music therapy is extremely similar to broad art therapy in that it transcends language itself. Simply hearing notes of a song you're listening to or even playing an instrument has shown that it helps you to regain a deeper connection to yourself. Music is multi-faceted; there is more than one way to experience the beauty and wonder of music as well as its power in healing. Studies have proven that sufferers of bulimia responded positively to music therapy and being able to reclaim their lives. According to music therapists Annika Lejonclou and Gro Trondalen, it helped patients with eating disorders '...empower the clients' strength, support inner healing resources and contribute to a living bridge between body and mind, which subsequently support healing resources and nourish hope of a normal life...' (2007). In addition to experimenting with new environments, you can experience music therapy on your own by going to concerts to see your favorite band, learning to play a new instrument, or simply listening to new genres of music. The idea is to not only remove any previous triggers but to experience a newfound love and appreciation for yourself.

Even with all the newness and implementation of new facets of your life, there will still be bumps in the road. There will be times the urge to purge will outweigh the want to do better, especially in the beginning. The most important aspect of this chapter, aside from seeking help, is that it takes both time and patience for a full recovery.

TIME AND PATIENCE

Changing your life on your own takes an investment of time and even more patience. You want to get better and feel like yourself again in the least amount of time. Believe me, I was once where you are now. When I looked at myself in the mirror and saw myself as a shell of who I used to be, it was a wake-up call that my life needed to change.

No one overcomes a disorder in a day or even a week. It takes constant rebuilding of yourself and the drive to achieve recovery. There will be times that you may want to quit and regress to bulimia because it takes a lot out of you to implement these changes. Recovery requires a new outlook on life that you know you're ready for, but you're afraid of failing at recovery. There will be bad days ahead, especially when the stresses are so great it takes everything you have not to purge. Life isn't easy no matter how old you are. Life will knock you down and keep you down if you let it.

However, you have to keep pushing through to change your life. Applying these activities and mindset shifts slowly into your routine will help you more than if you were to completely change everything about you at once. I know that it's tempting, but the shock of a completely new lifestyle will do more harm than good. By taking small steps, you'll be able to slowly gain control of your routine, lifestyle, and eventually your mind and your relationship with food.

I know firsthand how frustrating it is to want to recover. This is why the language I use around the term 'recovery' refers to a long distance between two destinations. Your current situation is filled with fear, uncertainty, and the longing for change. The end destination is to be fully healed and not in the current headspace you're in. It may feel as though it's taking forever but think about the inner peace you'll have and the inner strength you'll build by taking the first steps to recovery.

I promise you, this will all be worth it in the end. Your future health and lifestyle are depending on you to take care of yourself and give your body the love, respect, and acceptance it needs. I care about your well-being for both your future and your current self. Be compassionate to yourself and ruthlessly take the steps you need for healing. You deserve it.

KEY TAKEAWAYS

I truly hope that the tips you've learned in this chapter will be guides on your trek toward a healthier, freer you. You deserve self-compassion and respect, and I hope with these tips you'll be able to find the best course of action for you. Here are the tips summarized for you as a refresher.

- Taking each step slowly and applying them will help you out more in the long run.
- Reframing your mindset is one of the key elements to battling this disorder. However, it's also one of the hardest to overcome.
- Practicing positive self-talk may seem silly at first, but it may help you shed light on your perceived flaws. This is one way to reframe your thinking about your body.
- Journaling, especially gratitude journaling, can help you focus more on the positives in your daily life. The more specific each event, the better.
- Getting help is one of the most crucial aspects of recovery. Getting professional help will make you better understand the nature of your disorder.
- One-on-one therapy is a great way for you to unpack your feelings and allow someone to guide you down a path to recovery.
- Group therapies are beneficial because it's the visual perception that you're not alone. Listening to others talk about their struggles will make you feel less isolated.

- Positive extracurricular activities will help boost your self-confidence and allow for imperfection.
- When you change your environment, you also begin to change with it. Trying new things or even getting back into the hobbies you used to enjoy will help regulate your emotions.
- Exercising outside the realm of your triggers and sports outside of school will also help you on the road to healing. With this type of exercise, you are free to stop when you want and also not have the weight of expectation placed on you.
- Meditation is a practical way of venturing inside your mind through yoga or other self-care exercises. It helps clear your mind as you practice self-awareness and self-reflection.
- Art and music therapy unleash your creative side with the ability to express yourself in a way you usually can't.
- Time and patience are incredible and powerful values and virtues you will need to learn for your recovery to be successful and not fall into relapses. You are capable of fighting your inner voices by succeeding and achieving recovery.

However, you are the only one who can make this happen for you. Therapy, and the other tips that I suggested, will only work if you open yourself up to those possibilities. Don't allow your fear to prevent you from becoming who you were meant to be. It's stolen so much from you; don't let it steal your chances of becoming better.

AFTERWORD

You picked up this book because you knew it would contain information about overcoming bulimia. After finishing, you've learned so much about your disorder and how to implement the strategies to overcome it. While your recovery process will take so much time, effort, and patience, it will be worth it in the end.

Bulimia is a disorder that negatively affects your ability to hold onto and form new relationships, including the relationship you have with food. It is a cycle that's devastating to both your body and your health. However, your experiences are uniquely yours, and therefore, only you have the power to change them.

YOUR CURRENT STATUS

Within this book, you've learned valuable information that can help you understand the disorder itself, how it affects you and your relationships, and how to build the foundation for recovery. In the first chapter, we discussed what exactly bulimia is: an eating condition that stems from a loss of control in your life by consuming foods and then excessively purging. There are many underlying causes for the disorder including your genetics, environment, and social pressures to be skinny. You have trouble regulating your emotions.

The second chapter discussed how bulimia is your crutch to the pressures of daily life. As academic and social pressures mix, they can create a negative swirl of emotions such as guilt, shame, and secret keeping. Due to your shame, you feel as though you must keep your disorder a secret to prevent an outcome you fear. Bulimia becomes your 'dirty little secret', adding to the dead weight of food in your body in addition to the need for secrecy.

The third chapter has given you the tools to study and understand your role within the family. Your family system and the power dynamics within your family cause excessive guilt and the weight of expectations on your shoulders. After you internalize the comments made to you by the people closest to you, it's difficult to see yourself from another perspective. This detachment from your family creates self-imposed isolation.

In Chapter 4, the discussion revolved around your friend group and the pressures of society and media as a whole. Your friends ignore the increasingly obvious problem that's arising in front of them. You dread socialization, but you often feel guilty about the slow withdrawal from them. Portrayals of thin, pretty actresses illustrate the pressures of society on adolescents and teenagers. Teenagers believe that to be successful, they must be skinny and beautiful.

The fifth chapter introduces and explains the concepts of your current extracurricular activities. It also explains how your environment can either positively or negatively impact your mental health and well-being. Some of these activities promote bulimia and withdrawal. Even though there are many occasions revolving around your extracurricular that are cause for celebration, these same occasions skew your perception of your body. The disappointing moments can lower you even more because of how you view yourself. You want to fit in, but the harsh lens of your self-perception can deepen your feelings of isolation and withdrawal.

While it may seem that your own body and mind have betrayed you, there are steps you can actively take to free yourself from the prison of bulimia. Because you've picked up this book for help, I know you're on the right path toward healing.

YOUR PATH TO HEALING

The last chapter of this book discusses hope and gives you concrete, actionable steps to overcome this disorder. Because bulimia is a tricky disorder at best, the necessary steps for you to overcome this chapter in your life will be small. These small steps, however, are necessary for your success. The first step is to reframe your mindset about yourself and your body. Journaling and practicing positive self-talk can help you reframe your negative mindset into a more positive one over time.

Remember, there is no weakness in asking for help, only strength. Receiving help can be in the form of going to group or one-on-one therapies, but the main goal is to find your support system to both guide you and hold you accountable for your recovery. A support system of family and friends is wonderful. Add to the list an expert and others who have struggled with bulimia, and you'll have an unstoppable force of love and support that you'll need.

In addition to reframing your mindset and the amazing support system aligned in your recovery process, there are also positive outlets you can experience as well. Trying out new things, experimenting with new environments, and reclaiming old hobbies will help you climb out of the depths that bulimia has thrown you in. Dabbling in art and music as well as meditating on yourself and your world will open your mind to the possibilities.

WHAT WILL YOU DO?

Now that you've finished reading this book, how do you feel? Do you feel empowered to close this chapter in your life and start writing a new one? You now have all the tools you need to start making changes to your life today. In your journal, write down three goals you want to accomplish by the end of the week. What those goals are will be determined by you. Maybe you want to implement a round of meditation or even talk to a trusted adult.

I know the path you're about to take can be hard, but your life and health are precious. You deserve the path to recovery, and I know you have the determination and drive to make it happen for you. As long as you're making progress, that's all that truly matters on your journey. It will be brutal at first, but you must persevere. Make your recovery a priority.

I promise you, it will become easier. This chapter of your life will end, and you will reclaim your life and happiness.

You have the tools you need to succeed. Now, it's time to use them. Your future self will thank you.

BIBLIOGRAPHY

20 Popular Drinks That Cause Stomach Bloating. (n.d.). Diet.St. Retrieved July 26, 2022, from https://www.diet.st/5-popular-drinks-that-cause-stomach-bloating/

Benninghoven, D., Schneider, H., Strack, M., Reich, G., & Cierpka, M. (2003). Family representations in relationship episodes of patients with a diagnosis of bulimia nervosa. Psychology and Psychotherapy: Theory, Research and Practice, 76(3), 323–336. https://doi.org/10.1348/147608303322362532

Canada, L. and A. (2019, March 8). Search—Theses Canada. https://www.bac-lac.gc.ca/eng/services/theses/Pages/item.aspx?idNumber=1032961144

Ciccolo, E. B. F. (2008). Exploring Experience of Family Relations by Patients with Anorexia Nervosa and Bulimia Nervosa Using a Projective Family Test. Psychological Reports, 103(1), 231–242. https://doi.org/10.2466/pr0.103.1.231-242

Copetti, A. V. S., & Quiroga, C. V. (2018). The influence of media on eating disorders and the self-image in adolescents. Revista de Psicologia Da IMED, 10(2), 161–177. https://doi.org/10.18256/2175-5027.2018.v10i2.2664

Eid, M., & Larsen, R. J. (2008). The Science of Subjective Well-Being. Guilford Press.

Erriu, M., Cimino, S., & Cerniglia, L. (2020). The Role of Family Relationships in Eating Disorders in Adolescents: A Narrative Review. Behavioral Sciences, 10(4), 71. https://doi.org/10.3390/bs10040071

Espeset, E. M. S., Gulliksen, K. S., Nordbø, R. H. S., Skårderud, F., & Holte, A. (2012). The Link Between Negative Emotions and Eating Disorder Behaviour in Patients with Anorexia Nervosa. European Eating Disorders Review, 20(6), 451–460. https://doi.org/10.1002/erv.2183

Gonçalves de Oliveira, A.P., et. al. Eating disorders, body image and media influence in university students. J Nurs UFPE on line. 2020. https://periodicos.ufpe.br/revistas/revistaenfermagem/article/viewFile/245234/35656

Khodabakhsh, M. R., & Kiani, F. (2014). Effects of Emotional Eating on Eating Behaviors Disorder in Students: The Effects of Anxious Mood and Emotion Expression. International Journal of Pediatrics, 2(4.1), 295–303.

Lecomte, A., Zerrouk, A., Sibeoni, J., Khan, S., Revah-Levy, A., & Lachal, J. (2019). The role of food in family relationships amongst adolescents with bulimia nervosa: A qualitative study using photo-elicitation. Appetite, 141, 104305. https://doi.org/10.1016/j.appet.2019.05.036

Lejonklou, A., & Trondalen, G. (2009). "I've started to move into my own body": Music therapy with women suffering from eating disorders. Nordic Journal of Music Therapy, 18(1), 79–92. https://doi.org/10.1080/08098130802610924

Linardon, J., Phillipou, A., Castle, D., Newton, R., Harrison, P., Cistullo, L. L., Griffiths, S., Hindle, A., & Brennan, L. (2018). Feeling fat in eating disorders: Testing the unique relationships between feeling fat and measures of disordered eating in anorexia nervosa and bulimia nervosa. Body Image, 25, 163–167. https://doi.org/10.1016/j.bodyim.2018.04.001

Lut. (n.d.). Emotion Awareness and Identification Skills in Adolescent Girls With Bulimia Nervosa: Journal of Clinical Child & Adolescent Psychology: Vol 33, No 4. Retrieved July 29, 2022, from https://www.tandfonline.com/doi/abs/10.1207/s15374424jccp3304_11

Lutz, A. P. C., Dierolf, A., van Dyck, Z., Georgii, C., Schnepper, R., Blechert, J., & Vögele, C. (2021). Mood-induced changes in the cortical processing of food images in bulimia nervosa. Addictive Behaviors, 113, 106712. https://doi.org/10.1016/j.addbeh.2020.106712

Martin, K., Woo, J., Timmins, V., Collins, J., Islam, A., Newton, D., & Goldstein, B. I. (2016). Binge eating and emotional eating behaviors among adolescents and young adults with bipolar disorder. Journal of Affective Disorders, 195, 88–95. https://doi.org/10.1016/j.jad.2016.02.030

Mayo Clinic Staff. (2022). Bulimia nervosa—Symptoms and causes. Mayo Clinic. https://www.mayoclinic.org/diseases-conditions/bulimia/symptoms-causes/syc-20353615

Mayo Clinic Staff. (2022). Eating disorders—Symptoms and causes. Mayo Clinic. https://www.mayoclinic.org/diseases-conditions/eating-disorders/symptoms-causes/syc-20353603

McCabe, M. P., Ricciardelli, L. A., & Ridge, D. (2006). "Who Thinks I Need a Perfect Body?" Perceptions and Internal Dialogue among Adolescents about Their Bodies. Sex Roles, 55(5), 409–419. https://doi.org/10.1007/s11199-006-9093-0

McLead, S. (n.d.). Maslow's Hierarchy of Needs | Simply Psychology. Retrieved August 6, 2022, from https://www.simplypsychology.org/maslow.html

Meule, A., Richard, A., Schnepper, R., Reichenberger, J., Georgii, C., Naab, S., Voderholzer, U., & Blechert, J. (2021). Emotion regulation and emotional eating in anorexia nervosa and bulimia nervosa. Eating Disorders, 29(2), 175–191. https://doi.org/10.1080/10640266.2019.1642036

Murn, L. T. (2010). Group Therapies for the Treatment of Bulimia Nervosa. Inquiries Journal, 2(12). http://www.inquiriesjournal.com/articles/336/group-therapies-for-the-treatment-of-bulimia-nervosa

Quadflieg, N., & Fichter, M. M. (2003). The course and outcome of bulimia nervosa. European Child & Adolescent Psychiatry, 12(1), i99–i109. https://doi.org/10.1007/s00787-003-1113-9

Russell, G. (1979). Bulimia nervosa: An ominous variant of anorexia nervosa. Psychological Medicine, 9(3), 429–448. https://doi.org/10.1017/S0033291700031974

Sansone, R. A., & Sansone, L. A. (2010). Gratitude and Well Being. Psychiatry (Edgmont), 7(11), 18–22.

Santos, T., Marques, C., Pereira, A., Soares, S., & Macedo, A. (2018). Family systems, offspring and eating disorders: Can perfectionism close the gaps? 5, 1–8. https://doi.org/10.21035/ijcnmh.2018.5.6

Saunokonoko, A. J., Mars, M., & Sattmann-Frese, W. J. (2022). The significance of the father-daughter relationship to understanding and treating Bulimia Nervosa: A Hermeneutic Phenomenological Study. Cogent Psychology, 9(1), 2095721. https://doi.org/10.1080/23311908.2022.2095721

Schlachter, K. (n.d.). The Great Hunger: Understanding and Treating Adolescent Eating Disorders.

Schnepper, R., Richard, A., Georgii, C., Arend, A.-K., Naab, S., Voderholzer, U., Wilhelm, F. H., & Blechert, J. (2021). Bad mood food? Increased versus decreased food cue reactivity in anorexia nervosa and bulimia nervosa during negative emotions. European Eating Disorders Review, 29(5), 756–769. https://doi.org/10.1002/erv.2849

Shatkin, J. P. (2020). Increasing Access for the Treatment of Eating Disorders Among College Students. JAMA Network Open, 3(8), e2016117. https://doi.org/10.1001/jamanetworkopen.2020.16117

Sim, L., & Zeman, J. (n.d.). Negative emotion-related eating behaviours in young women with underweight status, overweight status, anorexia nervosa, and bulimia nervosa in Korea—An—2022—European Eating Disorders Review—Wiley Online Library. Retrieved July 29, 2022, from https://onlinelibrary.wiley.com/doi/abs/10.1002/erv.2900

Slater, A., & Tiggemann, M. (2015). Media Exposure, Extracurricular Activities, and Appearance-Related Comments as Predictors of Female Adolescents' Self-Objectification. Psychology of Women Quarterly, 39(3), 375–389. https://doi.org/10.1177/0361684314554606

The Treatment of Eating Disorders: A Clinical Handbook—Google Books. (2010). https://books.google.com/books?hl=en&lr=&id=wEuK3Tlh-POoC&oi=fnd&pg=PA271&dq=bulimia+nervosa+teens+talking+to+family+isolation&ots=TOxY4PV-ZL&sig=uaQHKxdlWJY6kaz_1nC04J0te00#v=onepage&q&f=false

Trauma and shock. (n.d.). Https://Www.Apa.Org. Retrieved August 2, 2022, from https://www.apa.org/topics/trauma

Twardowski-Deskin, J. (2020, December 15). Exploring the Lived Experience of Sisters of Women Diagnosed with Bulimia Nervosa: A Qualitative Case Study - ProQuest. https://www.proquest.com/openview/83-dae434cde536bcdd1c82daa3ed7e7d/1?cbl=18750&diss=y&pq-origsite=gscholar

Valdanha-Ornelas, É. D., Squires, C., Barbieri, V., & Santos, M. A. dos. (2021). FAMILY RELATIONSHIPS IN BULIMIA NERVOSA. Psicologia Em Estudo, 26. https://doi.org/10.4025/psicolestud.v26i0.47361

van Strien, T., van der Zwaluw, C. S., & Engels, R. C. M. E. (2010). Emotional eating in adolescents: A gene (SLC6A4/5-HTT) – Depressive feelings interaction analysis. Journal of Psychiatric Research, 44(15), 1035–1042. https://doi.org/10.1016/j.jpsychires.2010.03.012

Welch, S. L., Doll, H. A., & Fairburn, C. G. (1997). Life events and the onset of bulimia nervosa: A controlled study. Psychological Medicine, 27(3), 515–522. https://doi.org/10.1017/S0033291796004370

Wiesmann, M. (2022, June 27). Does the use of social media mediate the relationship between bulimia nervosa and orthorexia nervosa in university students? [Info:eu-repo/semantics/bachelorThesis]. University of Twente. http://essay.utwente.nl/90895/

Wolfe, W. L., & Patterson, K. (2017). Comparison of a gratitude-based and cognitive restructuring intervention for body dissatisfaction and dysfunctional eating behavior in college women. Eating Disorders, 25(4), 330–344. https://doi.org/10.1080/10640266.2017.1279908

Zhou, X. (2019). An exploration of the core conflictual relationship theme (CCRT) in the mother-daughter relationship among patients with bulimia nervosa and healthy controls [Dissertation, Universität Ulm]. https://doi.org/10.18725/OPARU-11762